The Lean-To-Boys of Bigfork, Minnesota

The Deer and Bear Hunting, Adventures and Traditions of the Lean-To-Boys in Minnesota; Including, Idaho Elk hunting.

Charlie Turnbull

Copyright © 2013 Charlie Turnbull
All rights reserved.

ISBN: 1490498710
ISBN 13: 9781490498713

DEDICATION

I have dedicated this book to
Clarence E. Sjodin
1909-1966

Clarence hunted with us from 1952 to 1962. He was our mentor, my friend and Junior's Dad. His guidance and teaching have been a meaningful part of our lives and in the success we have had in over 60 years of deer hunting in Bigfork, Township, Itasca County, Minnesota.

TABLE OF CONTENTS

Acknowledgements vii

Introduction: ix

1:	The Lean-To-Boys of Bigfork	Charlie Turnbull	1
2:	My Big Buck	Bob Nelson	15
3:	Our Lost Years of Deer Hunting	Charlie Turnbull	25
4:	The 1955 Minnesota Deer Hunt	Junior Sjodin	32
5:	Deer Hunting in 1956	Pete Wojciechowski...........	43
6:	Too Much Snow in '57	Charlie Turnbull	49
7:	My First Big White Tail	Charlie Turnbull	52
8:	One Cold Year	Doug Mitchell	58
9:	Romantic Ideas versus Cold Reality	Marlene Turnbull..............	62
10:	Creation of a "Swamp Buggy"	Junior Sjodin	69
11:	Unsolicited Publicity	Western Itasca Review.......	78
12:	The Early 1960s	Charlie Turnbull	81
13:	My Old Man	Junior Sjodin	87
14:	Another Big Buck Year	Charlie Turnbull	93
15:	Leaving a Pile of Entrails	Bob Sodman	97

16:	The Pre-hunt Meetings	Chuck Sjodin	106
17:	Paul's Excitement	Paul Sjodin	111
18:	Bigfork Bear Hunting	Charlie Turnbull	118
19:	The Buck King	Punky Sjodin	124
20:	Terry and Her Bear	Terry Turnbull Leadabrand	135
21:	Hunting, Frustration & Redemption	Jim Smith	147
22:	The Lean-To-Boys Take Up Elk Hunting	Charlie Turnbull	151
23:	Women and the Lean-To-Boys	Charlie Turnbull	163
24:	New in Camp	Steve Quade	179
25:	Deer Camp Fare	Vince Turnbull	186
26:	A True Bird Hunter	Steve Sjodin	194
27:	Stands	Charlie Turnbull	202
28:	Shelters for the Lean-To-Boys	Charlie Turnbull	208
29:	Every Camp Needs an Outhouse	Charlie Turnbull	217
30:	The Evolution of Our Means of Travel	Charlie Turnbull	221
31:	Over 60 Years of Recollections	Junior Sjodin	228
32:	2012 Minnesota Deer Harvest Report	Minn. DNR	236

ACKNOWLEDGEMENTS

I want to thank all the Lean-To-Boys for their cooperation and for the stories they told or wrote for this book. My friends who read the early manuscripts and gave me invaluable feedback, they too need to be thanked. They include Linda Baker, Allan Powell, Mary Anne VandeVusse, Jean Flicker, Junior Sjodin, and my wife, Marlene Turnbull.

Several years ago, Anita Apley advised me of an upcoming writer's workshop. She encouraged me to attend. It helped me get started with my writing.

Two other people also helped me with information that I needed Leslie McInenly, Minnesota Dept. of Natural Resources, with information on deer and bear hunting, and Britta Arnedt, editor of the Grand Rapids Herald Review, for her help in tracking down the newspaper article used in Chapter 11.

The final push, to complete the book, to have it right, required more editing than I could do; my friend, Blair Kooi came to my rescue. I also owe him a big Thank You.

Without the help and encouragement I received from my friends and family this collection of stories may not have been written. I owe them all a big thank you.

Charlie Turnbull

The Lean-To-Boys of Bigfork, Minnesota

INTRODUCTION

This book is about two men, their families and friends. These men were raised in families that have strong hunting traditions. They love hunting, fishing, camping and a wide variety of outdoor activities.

In the stories, you will see how that tradition has been passed on within and between their families. Also, how they have shared, encouraged and included others in their deer hunting and outdoor activities, and how they created, used and have maintained their deer hunting camp in Bigfork Township, Itasca County, Minnesota since 1952.

The camp provides the setting for over 60 years of deer hunting and related stories. In addition it touches on how their camp and the area they use for deer hunting has become the base for an expanded range of outdoor opportunities.

The mutual friendship between the two families started in the late 1940s. After WW II, Junior was a golf course "hustler," and so was I. By hustler, I mean we searched for lost golf balls in the roughs, creeks and ponds at various golf courses in, or around Minneapolis.

This was after WW ll, back in 1946 and 1947. It was a time when golf balls were scarce and expensive. Once balls were found, selling them, back to golfers, provided us with spending money. Junior, along with his friend Fred, worked the Theodore Wirth Public Golf Course. My friends, the Johnson brothers, and I worked the Meadow Brook Public Golf Course.

In the spring of 1947, my family moved from Minneapolis to Constance, about 25 miles north of the Twin Cities. We became city farmers on 200 acres in Anoka County. My chances to go "roughing and diving" for golf balls became almost nonexistent.

I did have one more chance in the summer of 1947. I hitchhiked to the Twin Cities and met up with the Johnson brothers. Then we drove out to Meadow Brook where Minnehaha Creek runs through the 14th and 16th fairways. Usually, this meant lots of golf balls could be found by swimming in the creek. Not so that day.

One of the Johnson brothers said, "Let's go to Theodore Wirth where they have ponds and water holes." Theodore Wirth seemed like a good idea. It was, until the golf course "Ranger" at Theodore Wirth found us swimming for golf balls. He escorted us, as trespassers, up to the clubhouse to wait for the police.

As it turned out, we were not the only ones in the same predicament. Two others were also picked up for the same reason. One of us got to talking to the other two, and found out that one of them had a revolver in his possession.

All we knew at that time was, when the police officer came, he was very startled when this other kid took out, of his pocket, a revolver. The police officer, after jumping back, detained the other two, and then the Ranger walked the Johnsons and me to our car and searched it. He confiscated the dozen or so golf balls we had and told us to never come back. End of story as we knew it.

Two years later, Junior's family moved to Anoka County. We met at Anoka High School. Over time, we shared various stories about hunting and hustling golf balls. Junior told me about his friend Fred and a revolver incident they had at Theodore Wirth golf course. I knew immediately that our paths had crossed in the summer of 1947.

As we talked, we also found we had similar interests in many areas, especially hunting and fishing.

Junior shot his first deer, up in the Leech Lake area, when he was a junior in high school. The four years I lived on the farm, I was deer hunting and I was still looking for my first.

In 1951, Junior, Pete and I tried the Buck Hill and Crystal Lake area just south of the Twin Cities. For us, it was a losing proposition. Junior's dad, Clarence, heard about it and said, "We're going DEER HUNTING up NORTH" in 1952! He said it's too dangerous hunting south of Minneapolis.

Chapter 1

THE LEAN-TO-BOYS OF BIGFORK, MINNESOTA OR IN THE BEGINNING

Charlie Turnbull

Surprisingly, for the second day of Minnesota's 1952 deer season, it was unseasonably warm. It was a great day to be deer hunting in northern Minnesota. I was sitting high on a large rock pile overlooking a well-used deer trail.

That Sunday, it was easy to enjoy the warmth and comfort of the morning sun. I was sitting there daydreaming and enjoying what a nice day it really was, and the brightly-shining sun was promising even more warmth.

While I was sitting there, my daydreaming came to an abrupt halt. The rustling of dry, noisy leaves on the trail below me caught my attention and put me on full alert. When I looked down, there was a deer. The deer, a buck, was right below me. He was less than 20 feet away. This was a big buck. He offered me the opportunity, the shot, the one I had always been dreaming of taking.

With my heart pumping fast and my adrenaline overflowing, I took aim. The crosshairs were focused on the buck's front shoulder. I held my breath and, as I was following the buck with my scope, I squeezed off a round.

The buck bolted and bounded to the left. Did I miss? At 20 feet, how could I? The buck should have dropped in his tracks. He did not.

My surprise and disappointment were immediate. Had I missed? This was the big buck I had read about in the outdoor magazines. It was the shot I had dreamed about and imagined I would be taking some day. Had I missed?

Had I missed? That was a very good question, one that needed an answer.

Before I even try to answer the questions about that opportunity, I need to put this 1952 hunt in its proper perspective. After all, this hunt was the first and the beginning of a longstanding hunting party and camp. This is a hunting party, one that has survived, and has been in existence over 60 years, and it is still viable.

My friends, Junior and Pete, and I had been doing a lot of pheasant, grouse, and duck hunting around my family's farm and other parts of Anoka County. The year we graduated from Anoka High School, Junior, Pete and I hunted deer in southern Minnesota.

We chose southern Minnesota for that hunt after I suggested an area south of the Minnesota River. Several years earlier, my stepfather and I had hunted the area around and east of Buck Hill. On that hunt, my stepfather harvested a doe on the east slope of Buck Hill. It was on the slope overlooking Crystal Lake. That slope is now part of the Buck Hill Ski Resort and Interstate Highway 35.

Our hunt in 1951 was not as successful. In fact, we were very disappointed. In one woods we did find some tracks. I did see one doe and I missed her when I took a shot with my Ithaca 20 gauge shotgun.

The hunting available in southern Minnesota at that time was a big disappointment. Another one of our concerns was our inability to use a rifle in the southern part of Minnesota. After hunting in southern Minnesota, we decided to go up north for the 1952 deer season.

With "up north" in mind, Junior and I, along with our dads started planning a 1952 hunt in northern Minnesota. Junior's dad, Clarence, in the late 1920s, had worked in the area north and east of Bigfork. In those days, Clarence worked in the lumber camps as a cat skinner and as a lumberjack.

Clarence worked as handler of horses for George Luchau, a supervisor at the lumber camp. Clarence was able to learn about Bigfork and Effie and the hunting and fishing that was available in the area. He thought some of his friends from the 1920s would still be living in the area, and he was sure they would be willing to give advice and help in finding a good area in which to hunt.

In August of 1952, my stepfather passed away. That put a crimp in the planning for the hunting trip. It was our feeling that a party of four would be ideal. We checked with Pete, and he couldn't take on a hunt that year. We started talking to our other friends about a 1952 deer hunt up north. Our hope was to have one of them joined with us for our planned hunting trip.

Most of our friends were somewhat interested. Finally, Bob committed to joining our hunting party. Bob had been a year ahead of us in high school. He also lived on a farm near my old family farm in Constance.

The farm Bob lived on bordered Mud Lake and Lehman Lake. We had hunted ducks with Bob and his brother, Dick, on those lakes, and several sloughs in the area. Junior and I knew Bob would be a good fit for our hunting party.

With our hunting party set at four, we needed to nail down an "up north" location. Clarence's idea about Bigfork was as promising as any. We started our planning by reviewing a State Map of Minnesota.

The small town of Bigfork is located at the confluence of the Rice River and the Big Fork River. Its location in Itasca County is west of where the Mississippi River starts. Grand Rapids is 40 miles south and Effie is 11 miles north of Bigfork.

Itasca County is known as one of the better counties for hunting deer, bear and grouse. The county, because of its many lakes, is also known for its good fishing.

Clarence also mentioned the small town of Craig (also known as Craigsville.) Craig is located two miles north of Effie. Clarence told us that, back in the 1920s, Craig was a booming town and catered to the "needs" of the loggers. He further said it was in Craig where he first heard a woman cussing. Back in those days, to the loggers, Craig was known as a wide open town. In Craig, Clarence, in the mid-1920s, as a young man, had his eyes abruptly opened at an early age of his life.

Benhart Rajala (deceased) of the Effie/Bigfork area in his book 'Tim-BERRR!' volume #1 has a glowing account of the "hay days" of Craig and how it provided for the "needs" of the lumberjacks through the late 1940s. When we saw it in 1952, Craig was a ghost town.

By checking various county maps we found a good share of the land was owned by the county, state or federal government. This meant almost anywhere we would want to hunt, access was easily available. The more we checked into the area the better it looked.

We still needed to plan an exploratory trip to Bigfork. It is one thing to review maps; they did give us a start but a site visit to the area was needed. The four of us decided to go to Bigfork early in September. We wanted to make sure we liked the area and would be able to set up a camp in November.

Based on the background information we found, and also our need to see the area, we planned a road trip to Bigfork. Dates early in September were chosen. Because of work commitments, Bob could not make the trip. The scouting trip for the rest of us was taken on a beautiful Saturday in early September.

The day we left, the sun was shining. By the time we reached Bigfork, the temperature was in the middle 70s. As we drove along one of the Itasca County Roads, one of the first things we saw was a big whitetail buck. He just stood there standing alongside the road. For several minutes, he watched us and we watched him. He finally turned and walked away. We took that as a good sign.

Clarence had told us about the logging camp cook and camp hunter whose name was "Buck" Larson. If Buck was still alive, Clarence knew he would help us find a place to hunt and camp. In Bigfork, we only had to ask one or two people to learn that Buck was still alive and living in the north end of town.

Clarence had told us that Buck could not hear. He communicated through written memos. As the logging camp cook, he regularly would bring back two or three deer each week for camp meat. Clarence knew Buck's inability to hear was not a hindrance to his ability to hunt.

It was easy to find Buck's home on the north end of Bigfork. The good thing about it, he was home. After introductions, he and Clarence reminisced about their working together in the logging camp.

Clarence told him about "us boys" looking for a place to hunt. That got Buck started telling us the story about the deer he shot the year before. He explained how the buck was standing in his garden. He shot it right from his back door with his shotgun and slugs.

Clarence finally got around to asking Buck about areas where we could hunt in November. He explained to Buck that we were looking for a good place for deer hunting. We also needed a place where we would be able to set up a camp for our hunting party.

Buck immediately agreed to show us the area he would recommend. Before we could go looking for a place to hunt and camp, he insisted that we have lunch before we headed out.

Buck offered us a "fare" of creamed peas on toast for lunch. We accepted his offer. Creamed peas on toast were not an everyday fare. It turned out to be a very tasty lunch. With lunch behind us, we were ready to go.

With Buck pointing the way, we headed south through Bigfork. On the south side of town, he had us head east on the road going past Our Lady of the Snows Church, the hospital and the cemetery. We went east, then north, then east, then north, then east. At each turn, the road became narrower, rougher and showed the signs of dried-up water holes.

The last turn was east on to a logging road. It was a better road than the one we had just traveled. The road that is marked with a "minimum maintenance road" sign definitely could have used some maintenance.

The logging road was an old road traveling through part of the Smith Property. Later, Jim Smith told us this logging road was the one that the school bus used when he was going to school in Bigfork. After a quarter of a mile we entered county owned land.

We continued on for another half mile. At that point we had to stop because we had reached Rice Creek. There was no bridge over the creek. The logging road, however, did continue in an easterly direction.

During the logging era the area immediately west of the creek was the site of a lumber mill and lumberjack camp. We parked on the old mill site.

Back in 1952 several slab and sawdust piles were still visible in the area. They were vivid reminders of the logging activity in the area, probably in the late 1940s. The previous era, the one of the 1920s was long ago.

Clarence had been a participant of that era as a young man. Poplar and pine trees were starting to emerge but had not yet taken over the landscape. Rice Creek was flowing north to its confluence with the Big Fork River.

We further explored the lumber mill site and the surrounding area. We found several other logging roads and trails going south and north from the road we were hiking.

Abandoned log cabins were found throughout the area. In 1952 when we saw them they were beyond repair. The roofs of the cabins were caved in and most of the logs were in a severe state of decay. It was our feeling they would not be suitable for our camp.

They, too, were remnants of the past. It was easy to imagine, back in their day, the cabins being used by the local lumberjacks and trappers, as they harvested the bounties the land provided. The cabins were a reminder of an earlier way of life and the kind of people living in the woods near Bigfork and Effie.

As we ventured along the logging roads we were amazed how we could look over the tops of the new pine and poplar trees. New trees had started to grow and were now reforesting the more recently logged off areas.

The vegetation was lush, the creek was flowing, and the woods were in good condition. As we explored further the stumps with 36 to 60 inch diameters were evident throughout the woods. They were the evidence left by the lumberjacks 10 to 40 years earlier.

This was an area we immediately liked. It conjured up dreams for Junior and me for the future and memories of an earlier life for Clarence and Buck.

Earlier Clarence had told us, if we could find Buck he would show us the best area for deer hunting. We found Buck and he did direct us to a great deer hunting area. Our expectations were more than met.

On this road trip we identified our "Up North" hunting area. The hunting party was now set at four; we also had identified our up north location for our first Bigfork hunt. With more enthusiasm than planning we were set to go.

We only had eight more weeks to go until we would again be heading north. When you are only 18 or 19 you can easily get psyched up and excited when it comes to hunting. For me this was especially true when it came to deer hunting.

Waiting for the hunt to start was driving me nuts. Time seemed to stands still. I wanted the clock to move faster. The eight weeks between our September visit and the start of the hunting season in November seemed to take forever.

Prior to leaving for Bigfork we had to plan several things. We knew where we were going. Food supplies, what cars we would drive and how we would sleep all needed our attention.

We had put together a basic list of food for our five days of hunting and camping. The menu and food list were fairly simple; eggs, pancakes, flour, bacon, hamburger, peanut butter, jelly and several loaves of bread were all included. Clarence made sure we had plenty of beer. I made sure we had plenty of milk.

The area of planning for our sleeping arrangements could have been better. We elected to build a lean-to for our shelter. What that means is that we brought with us a small piece of canvas to put over logs that we would prop up by leaning them on a crossbar. The crossbar would be tied to a couple of trees. Everybody was supposed to bring their own bedding.

Finally it was time to head north to Bigfork. Our plan was to take two cars. Bob drove his 1946 Ford convertible and picked up Clarence as his passenger. I would ride with Junior in his 1941 Plymouth. We were finally on our way.

On the way north Clarence had to make a few stops. Every hour or two he had to have a "shot" of whiskey with a beer chaser. Considering it was a four hour trip those stops were okay.

We also stopped in Grand Rapids and had a midmorning breakfast at Mickey's cafe. We only had 40 more miles left to reach Bigfork and our proposed hunting grounds.

The last 40 miles on Highway 38 were up one hill and down another. If we weren't going up or down a hill we were going around one curve or another. One thing about Itasca County, it has a lot of lakes and many curves in their roads. The State and County wound the roads around the lakes.

Everything on the trip north went well. We even made it all the way to the creek without incident.

That night when it came time to hit the sack we really found out how poorly we had planned our sleeping arrangements. Bob and Junior had brought a blanket or two. I however had a brand new sleeping bag. We decided to open the sleeping bag and lay it flat on the ground.

That worked out, what didn't work out were the blankets. The blankets were too small and not enough of them to adequately cover three 200 pound 6'1" young males.

Clarence had opted to sleep in the Plymouth. Obviously he had the best shelter of the four of us. In addition to a couple of blankets he could close the windows and keep his body heat in the car.

By morning the three of us in the lean-to were thoroughly chilled. By the time we were dressed, and had eaten, the sun was shining through the trees. It promised to be another sunny and warm day.

We needed that nice of a day on the Friday before the opening of the deer season. The first thing to do after a cold nights rest was to get warmed up. Second we needed to further explore the area.

Travel and making camp took most of Thursday. Friday we had a breakfast of bacon, eggs, and pancakes and of course milk and coffee. Finally after breakfast we were ready to further explore the area.

On the way to our camping area we had seen one trail that looked very promising. On Friday we followed it and discovered that it was a survey line that ran in a north/south direction. It was a natural 15 foot shooting lane right in the middle of the woods.

From our logging road you could walk approximately 3/4th mile south on the survey line. At that point it crossed the creek. The creek angled in an easterly direction. It did not flow totally north and south as we had earlier thought.

When we walked the survey line we found three or four deer trails that crossed it. This was one area we would want to use sometime during our hunt. All we needed was a chair or log to sit on.

Bob spent time checking an area close to our campsite. He and Junior found an open knoll less than ¼-mile from our camp. It too had several deer trails that crossed one another. There were several stumps nearby, ones he could sit on as he watched the trails.

The area appeared to be one of the best we had found. Bob decided he would use one of those stumps to sit on that first morning. Clarence, Junior and I had decided to walk the logging roads on opening morning.

Opening morning, November 4, 1952, was finally here. After a year of thinking and planning a trip to hunt deer in northern Minnesota we were finally going to do it. We had an early breakfast. We started out from camp shortly after 6:45 AM.

Bob only had to walk several hundred yards east on the logging road from our camp. At that point there was a trail heading north. It was a short walk to the stump he had chosen to sit on that first morning. That was where he would be overlooking several deer trails and a small clearing.

He must've been on his stand by 6:55 AM. Junior planned to stay in the vicinity of the camp and probably work his way west. Clarence and I however headed further east on our logging road. When we came to a 'T' we took the road heading north.

The road heading north was fairly well sheltered from the sun. It was a logging road well shaded and covered with a bed of thick green moss. That morning the woods and red squirrels were quiet. Walking on the moss was like walking on a plush carpet.

We had traveled north about a ¼-mile when we heard a shot. The sound and direction of the shot had to have been Bob. It definitely was a shotgun. Clarence checked his watch it was 7:10 am.

Clarence and I were sure it had to be Bob who had taken the shot. To our left there was a small clearing and several large stumps. Clarence ran over and jumped up on a stump. If Bob had missed or had spooked other deer they might come crashing our way.

I left Clarence standing on his stump. I continued walking north on the logging road. The moss covering the road became thicker. I was walking quietly in a northerly direction. I had only traveled a short distance when I caught a movement to my right.

It was a deer with its head down. It appeared to be munching on grass. I stopped and watched it for a few moments. The deer lifted its head. That was when I knew the deer was a buck.

I started to raise my rifle so that I would be able to get a good shot. Then a crazy thing happened. To my surprise the buck turned toward the logging road and walked out, stopped and stood only 20 yards in front of me.

My first deer was going to be a six point buck. I took aim, fired, and watched the buck fall to the ground. At 7:15 AM, on opening morning I had my first deer. As luck would have it, it was a buck.

If Bob hit the deer he shot at, our licenses would be half filled. I walked back to where Clarence was standing on the stump. I told him that I had shot a buck.

Clarence, a man who had hunted, homesteaded and worked in road construction in Alaska was our camps most experienced hunter. That morning, Clarence became my mentor in field dressing the buck.

When we returned to camp, we found out that Bob did harvest a buck. The shot we heard was Bob and his 12 gauge shotgun. Junior who was hunting nearby went over and helped Bob field dress his buck.

Junior always tells the story of what he saw when he arrived to help Bob. There Bob was, shot gun in hand, aiming at the buck, standing guard over his buck watching for any movement. Junior reached down and put his finger in the hole in the deer's head and reassured Bob it was dead.

The rest of the morning on opening day we spent the time needed to drag our two deer to camp. Once we had that chore completed we took time for lunch. Over lunch we discussed how we would hunt that afternoon.

Bob stated he would walk the logging roads and explore the woods. Clarence said he would go and sit on the survey line. Junior and I also opted to walk logging roads.

That afternoon Bob saw several deer as he rambled through the woods. He did not have any opportunity to take a shot. Junior walked the logging roads heading east and north. Junior had a great opportunity to harvest a buck. He had a misfire with the rifle he was using.

The rifle was my Model 99, 300 Savage. We knew the rifle would occasionally misfire. Using the rifle was a poor decision on our part. It should have been fixed prior to our going up north.

Later, when I was in the Marines I learned about headspace in a rifle. I corrected the rifles head space when I returned home in 1956. Since that time many decades ago the rifle has worked perfectly.

Clarence took the logging road west and found the trail into the survey line. He found a nice knoll to sit on. He later mentioned that he had seen several deer cross the survey line. He just couldn't get a shot. On the other hand I had walked several logging roads but had not seen any deer.

The second day was another bright sunny day in Bigfork. Walking the logging roads was a pleasure. I headed out and went past where I had harvested my buck the day before. At the next "T" I took the logging road east. As I was walking east on the road it was gradually turning to the south. Now I was traveling in a southeasterly direction.

As I was walking I noticed on my left a major rock outcropping. I continued walking another 10 to 15 minutes. It was then that I noticed that the terrain had changed from woods and rocks to tall grasses. I liked the wooded areas best.

I turned around and started walking back. As I walked back I looked up and there standing in the middle of the road stood a buck. He was just standing there watching me walk towards him. As soon as I stopped he turned, he took a leap and was immediately lost in the woods.

Just maybe if I had been more alert I may have seen him first. I walked to where he had been standing in the road. He had been standing on a deer trail.

The buck had turned back in the direction he came from. I followed the trail into the woods. As I walked along the trail I came to the outcropping of boulders I had seen earlier. There was a flat spot about 10 feet above the deer trail. I crawled up to the flat spot and found a rock to sit on. I was able to sit there and started to enjoy the rest of the morning's sun.

I was sitting there no more than 10 minutes when I heard the rustling of leaves coming from the trail below my rock perch. Then I saw the buck, only 20 feet below me.

His nose was to the ground. He appeared to be following the trail and a does' scent. The buck passed right below me. From my perch I took aim. My cross hairs were centered on his front shoulder. The buck was moving slowly to my right. I was also following the buck with my scope. I squeezed off a round.

The buck bolted left and bounded away. Did I miss, how could that be? He should have fallen, not bolted.

I was left with that question. Did I miss? Again, I sought out Clarence. I needed him to help me find a blood trail or figure out what happened.

We found no hair, no blood trail or any evidence that I had hit the buck. We came to the conclusion after a thorough search that I had missed.

To figure out what happened Clarence had me crawl up on the boulder. I sat down on the rock where I was sitting when I took the shot. Clarence remained below and walked the trail. I told him to stop at the point where I thought the deer was when I shot. Clarence studied the area and found some answers.

On my side of the trail he found a 5 inch poplar tree with a bullet hole through it. Across the trail he found a second tree that had a piece of bark tore off of it and a bullet hole in it. The entry hole in the second tree was higher than the height of the deer.

The evidence was very clear. The tree on my side of the trail had a small entry hole and a larger exit hole. The tree on the far side of the buck had a larger entry hole. The mushroomed bullet made that second hole and tore some of the bark off the tree.

This is the answer to the begining question in this story. Did I miss that buck?

In analyzing the situation we came to the conclusion that I was shooting down at a 45° angle. The bullet entered the first tree approximately a foot above the deer. When the bullet exited the first tree it did not keep its downward course, it evidently leveled off and went over the back of the deer.

The basic problem was my concentration on the deer and not on the trees. It is an easy thing to do when your target is walking and you're following the animal in your sights. In simple terms, I had shot a second tree when my bullet sailed over the buck.

Later that day Bob and his 12 gauge shotgun again connected. He shot another buck not too far from the area where I missed one that morning. Again he had a nice sized buck.

That same day, Clarence again was hunting the survey line. Two days in a row he had seen several does crossing the survey line. Clarence, also, was using a shotgun and slugs; he didn't feel that he could get a good shot so he passed them up.

Based on his two experiences on the survey line he recommended that I sit on the survey line Monday morning. He said any shot would be a long one and my scope and rifle might be best.

Early Monday morning I was sitting on the survey line with my scoped rifle. Clarence had told me the approximate place to sit. I followed his advice. I was there for about an hour. Close to 8 AM I had a buck fawn stop and stand in the middle of the survey line. It was a successful 90 yard shot.

Our hunting party had our fourth deer. With four deer in hand we broke camp. By noon we were headed south toward home. We had found a great place to hunt. Four happy hunters were leaving Bigfork and dreaming of future hunts in northern Minnesota.

This is the only good photo; we have, from our deer hunt in 1952. The picture was taken after dark; right after our arrival home on November 6th 1952.

Chapter 2

MY BIG BUCK

Friendships can last a lifetime. When Bob told Junior and me that he would join us for our "up north" deer hunt in 1952, it was the start of a lifelong friendship. All three of us knew each other from high school in Anoka, Minnesota. Bob graduated from Anoka High School in 1950; Junior and I graduated in 1951.

What binds people together are having similar interests, mutual friends, getting together once in a while and doing things they all enjoy. Our "up north" deer hunt at Bigfork was the event that started our shared friendship, one that has lasted a lifetime.

This shared friendship evolved from our high school days and from our deer hunting experiences in 1952. Since that time, we have remained close friends for over 60 years.

The three couples, Bob and Shirley, Junior and Marilyn and Marlene and I have been getting together for New Year's since January 1, 1957. We have rotated between us which family would sponsor the three to four day get-together.

We went through the child bearing years, the child raising years, the empty nest years and then the grand parenting years. Now, we are enjoying the "body reconstruction" and pill-pushing years together.

Bob only hunted with the Lean-To-Boys that first year. Every hunter who has hunted with the Lean-To-Boys has heard the story about Bob's first buck.

He lives on as one of the founding fathers of our camp. In this chapter Bob puts into perspective his first "up north" deer hunt. It is a great story and it is important to have him tell the story.

Chapter 2
My Big Buck
Bob Nelson

Most likely you will not believe this story. My first Buck was a 10 pointer only 15 feet away. It was opening morning for Minnesota's 1952 deer hunt. Back in 1952 it was a rather warm November forth. The sun was shining, it was a day meant to be deer hunting and sitting on a stump overlooking a small clearing.

Before I go any further, how and why I became a deer hunter is important. As a kid I lived on a small Minnesota farm. The area was known as Constance, Minnesota. (It should still be "Constance" but somebody on the city council from Andover Township pushed through the name Andover.) I did the various kinds of hunting trapping and fishing that most of the farm boys in our area were doing.

It was a good life without too many demands. We hunted pheasants, ducks and grouse. At that time white-tailed deer were not plentiful in the Constance area. The trapping I did was for muskrats, weasels and pocket gophers. Our land had a lake on the north side and a smaller lake on the southeast corner. They were both good for duck hunting and trapping muskrats.

Anoka County is known for its sandy soil which is good for the pocket gophers but not for farming. The County awarded $.10 for each pair of pocket gopher front feet. It was a way for us as kids to make a few dollars during the summer.

I don't want to mislead you because I did do some deer hunting on the farm. My first deer hunt at the farm was not too successful. In fact it was downright embarrassing.

I had been hunting in our woods and in the first two hours I hadn't seen anything. I decided to walk up to the house for a bite to eat.

As I was walking out of the woods and starting to cross the alfalfa field I met a nice buck. He was on a dead run heading right for me. He was no more than 20 yards away. I immediately dropped my 12 gauge shotgun on the ground. That deer literally surprised and scared the hell out of me. I guess dropping my shotgun on the ground would probably be called 'Buck Fever'.

I never told the story to anybody, I didn't have to. My family took care of that. They were always ready to give me some "razzing." It always started out like, do you remember the time Bob threw his shotgun at the Buck? That's all it took to get the ribbing started. After 60 years it still comes up every once in a while.

At the end of our high school years my twin brother and I kept trying to become successful deer hunters. It just never happened. Hunting deer around our farm and on some of our neighbors land just wasn't that good. Well, maybe the problem was Dick and I; we were not good hunters at that time.

Back in the 1940s, 50s and 60s most of our neighbors did not put "No Trespassing" or no hunting signs on their property. That allowed us, in many ways, to hunt on the neighbor's property as well as our own land.

If for some reason they did not want us to hunt on their property they would just call us and ask us not to hunt on their land. For the most part we had the run of the land, woods and the swamps to do our hunting.

Just to the west of our farm there was an area that was semi-swampy. It supported a few more deer than we had around the farm. The land had fairly tall grasses, some higher wooded areas, lots of dead falls and many small waterholes. The waterholes were small, but when your foot dropped in one your socks and your feet got wet. In the early 1950s we would always see a few deer tracks but when we were hunting we seldom ever saw a deer. All said, prior to 1952, I was not a successful deer hunter.

As I said before I had tried a lot of hunting which included some deer hunting but I had never harvested a deer. When Charlie and Junior asked me to go "up north" with them it sounded like a good idea. They had explained to me that the three of us and Junior's dad, Clarence would make up a party of four. The area we were thinking of hunting would be around Bigfork, Minnesota. I knew nothing of the Bigfork area. I just knew it was way up north. Bigfork is located in Itasca County. Itasca County is where the Great River starts. More importantly it is known for the best deer hunting in Minnesota. The trip, at that time, sounded like a winner to me.

When Junior and Charlie approached me to go on this hunting trip it appeared that the Korean War was not drawing to a conclusion. It was clear to me that I would be drafted late in the year or early in 1953. This would be my last chance to hunt for the next two years. Junior and Charlie were a year younger. They might have missed the draft but they told me their plan was to join the Marines after January first.

By doing that they would "beat the draft." They kept saying they wanted one more deer hunt prior to enlisting. Thinking back I am not sure they beat the draft, they just controlled when they would leave for the service. The thought of military service was a big motivator for all three of us during the summer and fall of 1952.

Junior said Bigfork was the area where his dad, Clarence worked when he was a young man. He had been a logger in his teens and early twenty's. Based on Clarence's memories of the area, Junior said, we wanted to check out the Bigfork area; with that information a road trip to Bigfork was planned for September. Just before we were to leave for Bigfork I found I had to work that weekend.

Junior, Clarence and Charlie visited Bigfork and scouted out the area. After their return I met with them and they were all excited about an area east of Bigfork. They said logging roads were clear of brush, easy to walk, and they crossed each other throughout the area. They also said a creek for water and several campsite locations were also available. From what they said it all sounded good to me.

As I started to prepare for the deer hunt I decided my 12 gauge shotgun and slugs would have to do. My plan, however, was to use it, not throw it on the ground. I would hate to give people more "ammunition" to harass and rib me about later.

The north woods, for the most part, only allowed for short range shots, probably in the 25 to 50 yard range. That would work for me using a shotgun with slugs. As it turned out everything worked out very well and the shotgun and slugs were no problem.

In the 1950s and 1960s the required color for your hat and coat was red. If you were hunting deer in Minnesota 'red' was the color the law demanded. Most of us had purchased white army surplus hooded parkas and dyed them red. Mine lasted for years. They did have a problem with fading. As the parkas faded they would blend in with the trees and leaves. At that point the hunter lost the safety benefit of the red gear.

Clarence was a former lumberjack and he had his own ideas on the subject of red clothing. He wore a Lumber Jack's red and black checked shirt. It was not a legal garment for hunting. Clarence said, 'close enough'. Like I said his red and black plaid shirt wasn't legal but in Clarence's mind it was "close enough."

The day we headed from Anoka to Bigfork I drove my 1946 Ford convertible and Clarence rode with me. The second car was Junior's car. Charlie rode with Junior up to Bigfork.

Along the way Clarence liked to stop for a drink. He liked a shot of whisky served with a beer chaser. The drive took over four hours so the stops worked out okay. When we got to Bigfork and traveled over the minimum maintenance road it was already 1 AM Friday morning. We had been on the road over five hours. It proved to be a short night.

The logging road was next. It was better than the minimum maintenance road. As we were driving through the woods we came to an open field on the right. There were deer jumping all over the place. It was a good sign for all the hunting ahead of us. At least I saw it as a good sign. Beyond the open field we were back into the heavy timber.

We finally stopped at the creek. The creek was a challenge, there was no bridge. Clarence got out of the car and surveyed the situation. The creek had about a 2 foot drop and it was about five feet wide. Clarence decided we could get across.

He backed up Junior's car, lined it up with the place he wanted to hurtle the creek and revved up the motor. He floored the accelerator, took his foot off the brake, and started forward gaining speed. When he got to the creek he did hurtle it. It was more like a major bounce or two, than a nice smooth hurdle. Luckily, from what we could tell no damage was done to the car. We now had a car on both sides of the creek

We all piled in Junior's car and continued another mile on the logging road. We soon found an excellent spot to set up our hunting camp.

After unloading the gear we had in Junior's car we drove back to the creek. We transferred to Junior's car the rest of the gear we had left in my car. Having a car on both sides of the creek was very good. Later on when we needed it, a car was available for a drive to town.

By now it was after 3 AM. We wouldn't get much sleep that night. I asked Charlie where we were going to sleep tonight. Charlie nodded toward a big pine tree. We stretched out on the ground, with our blankets and slept under the big pine tree. Even though during the day the weather was in the 70s it still got cold at night. Our chilled bodies welcomed the sun the next morning.

At our campsite the next morning our first task was to build a lean-to shelter. The lean-to we built was a simple structure. It consisted of 10 foot poles leaning on a crossbar tied to two up right poles. Going back to my football days, it would be like leaning the poles on the crossbar of the football fields' goal posts. We found out several years later that other hunters started calling our party the Lean-To-Boys. The name Lean-To-Boys has stuck with us ever since the mid 1950s.

Friday was my first day to explore the area. I missed the trip in September. I needed to take a good look around the area we were going to hunt. I walked east and west on the logging roads. I went north and south through the woods. My immediate goal was twofold, first I needed to know the area, and second I wanted to find a place to hunt the next morning.

By the end of the day I felt very good. I knew a lot about the area, where the roads went and where I would sit opening morning. As luck would have it my spot to sit was less than 200 yards from our camp. It was east of camp and about 50 yards north. I had found a small path that led me from the logging road to a small clearing in the woods. The ground cover on the clearing was short brush and grasses. I had located a stump to sit on; it gave me a good view of the clearing and the place where two deer trails crossed.

Opening morning I was ready. After a good breakfast I left camp. I headed east on the logging road and I found my trail into the woods. I even found the stump on which I planned to sit. If I had wandered off and missed the stump I may not have been in a good position. The stump was only 10 or 15 yards from the deer crossing located within the clearing. Because of the trails and the crossing it was important to find the stump I had selected.

I had to take an early morning walk to my stand. It would be in the dark. I arrived at the clearing and found my stump by 6:45 am.

It was starting to lighten up in the East. As the minutes passed each one brought more light into the woods. By 7 AM I could see the clearing clearly. I was as ready as I ever would be that opening morning on November 4, 1952.

During the time I found my stump, sat down and waited for the sun to dawn my thoughts were, will a deer come by, can it see me and will it run? This is crazy, I thought, if I do see a deer will my 12 gauge and slugs be good enough. I also wasn't sure why I gave up working to go hunting. I guess I had all the hope, jitters and doubts that first morning out on my stand. My emotions were all scrambled up in my thinking.

At 7:10 AM, that opening morning of Minnesota's 1952 deer season, everything changed. I had been watching the four possible ways a deer might come on one of those trails. After looking to my right and then left I looked straight ahead. WOW, a 10 point buck was 15 feet away. He was just standing there staring at me. Then he and I had a staring contest. I was thinking if I'm lucky I might get a shot. I slowly lifted my 12 gauge shotgun, leveled it, maybe even aimed and pulled the trigger.

The deer that had been standing in front of me, to my surprise, fell. At least this time I took a shot. No more throwing the gun on the ground. You might say I was pleased with myself.

Now my doubts and questions changed to, what do I do now? I sat on the stump for several minutes. The deer stopped thrashing and kicking. Do I leave the deer and look for Junior, or wait for him? As I was running questions through my mind I stood guard over the buck.

Junior who was walking nearby heard the shot. We had agreed earlier to help each other if one of us was successful in harvesting a deer. As I was standing there guarding the deer, Junior came to my stand. The first thing I asked Junior, "Is the deer dead?" Junior looked at the deer's head, reached down and put his finger in the 1 inch hole between the eyes of the buck.

Junior looked up at me and answered, "Yes Bob, he is very dead." He also told me there was no need to stand guard. The deer was not going to run away. What a relief, everything was under control.

Junior helped me field dress the deer. The two of us were able to drag the deer back to camp. The buck was my first deer. Also, he is one of the largest deer I have taken in the 60 years I have successfully been hunting deer.

That first morning was as good as it gets. I had a very nice ten pointer and was very pleased with myself. Shortly after our return to camp Junior and I found out Charlie had harvested a six pointer. We were half filled with two days to go. The rest of Saturday I walked and explored the woods. I jumped several does and fawns, but I could never get a clear shot at any of them. By the end of the day I had walked 5 to 6 miles and I knew a lot more about the area we were hunting. It was as good as a first day can get.

On Sunday nothing happened like it did on Saturday. Charlie had missed a buck in the morning. Clarence who was hunting the survey line said he saw a few does but could not get a shot. He too, was using a shotgun and slugs. The deer were too far away. He did suggest that on Monday morning Charlie needed to sit on the survey line. Charlie was the only one with a scope on his rifle and it would be a fairly good shot for him.

After our lunch and a short break I found myself in the area where Charlie had missed a buck in the morning. I spotted a buck a short ways away. The buck crossed right in front of me as I was walking the logging road. I did not get a chance to take a shot. About that time I had been thinking I'd just go back to our lean-to, by the big pine tree, for the night.

I thought about it for a few minutes. I wasn't sure if the buck had seen me. I decided to sit down and wait a few minutes to see what would happen. To my surprise he came back and started walking across the logging road. This time I was ready. I took aim and shot. Now I had my second buck. Junior, Charlie and I had to drag the deer over a mile to our camp. By the time we reached camp it was pitch dark. Again it was the end of another perfect day.

The 1952 deer season was a great success. Charlie did sit on the survey line Monday morning. He harvested a buck fawn in the morning.

By noon we had packed our gear and were ready to head home. The four of us Clarence, Junior, Charlie and I were four happy hunters.

After the 1952 season I was drafted. I left Minnesota for an Army Camp in December. After two years I was discharged. When I returned home I married my wife Shirley. We raised a family of four. It was well-balanced, two boys and two girls. I never again hunted with the Lean-To-Boys. What happened is I started hunting with my father-in-law and later with other friends. I now hunt in northwestern Minnesota.

I did go up to Bigfork in October of 2009. Charlie as part of his preparation for this book invited over 20 people to come and share stories of their days in the Lean-To-Boys Camp. It was a good get-together. Seventeen of us showed up and shared the stories of some good and great hunts. It was a very different experience from our hunting back in 1952.

We were meeting in a cabin with a real roof and walls. It can sleep at least twelve or more hunters. It has a good wood stove for heat. The cabin is a far cry from the Lean-To days of long ago.

At this time in my life I'm not sure where I'll be deer hunting from year to year. I do know this, that if I ever want to, the door to the Lean-To-Boys Hunting Camp will be open and I will be welcome.

Chapter 3

OUR LOST YEARS OF DEER HUNTING (OR OUR MILITARY YEARS)

Charlie Turnbull

It is true we lost two or three years of deer hunting when we were drafted or enlisted in the United States Military Service. Not one of us ever regretted the time spent in the service. It all started in 1950 after the onset of hostilities in Korea.

The summer of 1950 was the start of the Korean War. The military draft had been reinstated. In Minnesota, National Guard units were using the Anoka High School gym for fitness training. They were still using the gym when the 1950/51 school year started in September.

Junior and I were high school seniors during the 1950/51 school year. For us making any decision about the military was not immediately up front. After the 1951 deer hunting season we started to take our military obligations more seriously. Junior, Bob and I all knew the 1952 deer hunt would be our last for 2 or 3 years. The military decision we had to make was now up front.

Bob received his draft notice in late November, 1952. He was not surprised, just disappointed that he had to leave for basic training just prior to Christmas. In January, Junior and I selected the end of the month to enlist in the Marine Corps.

Junior, as a married man, could only join the Corps on a two year reserve enlistment. From what I could tell he liked that better than a three year enlistment. As a single person I could enlist for three, four or six years. The decision was very simple. Three years was plenty for me.

My plan was to get back home as soon as I could to enjoy more Minnesota deer hunting. More Minnesota deer hunting than I would by being in the service an extra year or more. If I wanted to I always could, at a later time, extend my enlistment. I was sure I would never do that, and I didn't.

Bob and his twin brother headed for Army Boot Camp in December 1952. After Boot Camp, Bob ended up in Germany. His brother went west and spent his time in Okinawa, Japan. We did not see either of them till several years later.

On January 26, 1953, Junior and I, by train, headed for the Marine Corps Recruit Depot in San Diego, California. When we arrived in San Diego we saw what appeared to be green grass. At least it appeared to be grass.

It was just cement painted a lawn colored green. Coming from Minnesota we knew painted concrete was not grass. The next thing I noticed was the lack of urinals in the toilet areas. I finally saw a through on the bottom of a nice ceramic wall with a drain hole in the middle of it. Eliminating on a tiled wall was different too. My thought was, evidently they do things differently in Southern California.

When I entered boot camp I weighed 204 pounds. At the completion of the three months of boot camp they had me down to 192 pounds. Marching, calisthenics, jogging, and being on a strict and regimented Corps diet did it. From a health point of view it was a great three months.

The Corps sees every Marine first as a rifleman. Because of that every Marine is expected to become a qualified marksman with their rifle. That requirement the Corps has fit in perfectly with our personal interests.

We were issued M-1 rifles for our training. It was also our aid for calisthenics. Caring for the rifle was also high on the list for each Marine. At every inspection a D. I. or Lt. would inspect our rifles. It better not have a dirty bore or have dust on it. If it did you were in big trouble and ended up with extra clean-up duties.

In Boot Camp I did not do exceptionally well on the rifle range. I qualified, that was all. Junior on the other hand did very well; he qualified high, as an expert.

His score of 228 was the highest in our platoon of 70 Boots. To score expert you had to score between 220 and 250. To score a "possible" of 250 you would need to have 50 bull's eyes. Each shot counted 5 points. During my second and third years in the Marines I did score expert, it was just disappointing to do poorly in boot camp.

Boot camp certainly had its ups and downs. One incident stands out and we discuss it from time to time. We were cleaning our rifles and the rest of our gear in our Quonset huts. We were just taking it easy for a few minutes. All of a sudden the D. I. blew his whistle and his "top", so to speak.

We bolted out of our quarters and assembled on the parade grounds. As we were falling into formation the question was, now what? Our S.Sgt., D. I., marched one recruit from his office to the front of the platoon. He had him stand at attention facing the platoon. At that point the D. I. started berating the Boot. He started out by yelling at the rest of us Boots, "This Boot wants a transfer to the Navy. Do any of you other Boots want a transfer to the Navy?" The sarcasm was unquestionable. Needless to say not a one of the other 70 Boots stepped forward.

It was one of those situations where you are very happy that it was somebody else and not you standing in front of the platoon. On the positive side the person in question did stay in the Corps and graduated with our platoon. He had to put up with a lot of razzing. The razzing stopped as soon as somebody else "screwed up".

Some people had a true dislike for service life. Those of us who had backgrounds in hunting, camping, farming and/or other outdoors activities for the most part enjoyed the service.

Enjoying the service life did not mean loving it. Bob, Junior and I did not re-up at the completion of our enlistments.

In the early 1950s most of us who were in our late teens or early twenties were fairly patriotic. Therefore Bob, Junior and I just assumed we were going to join or be drafted into the military service. The alternative was to try and beat the draft. Some young men did this by going to college. To get this deferment they had to maintain their grades and stay in college.

Basically we didn't think much of people beating the draft. In our Boot Camp Platoon we had six or seven of the recruits who had been in college. They found, staying in college required work. It wasn't just a good place to go hide and have fun. When their college deferment was in jeopardy they opted to join the Marines. Obviously they had the background to get into college. They just weren't ready to do the work required to stay in school.

This turned out to be an eye-opener for me. Junior and I had scored in the upper 120s on the military service's General Qualifications Test. On an intellectual level we were up there with the best of them. With this information it was one of the first times I ever considered going to college.

I was aware that my three years in the Marines would guarantee me 36 months of post H. S. Education. The G.I. Bill, at that time gave you 1½ months of schooling for each month in active military service. The law had a cap of 36 months. Therefore my third year did not add any schooling benefits.

When Junior was discharged from the Marines in 1955 he took advantage of the education offered by the G.I. Bill. He attended a major vocational school and specialized in welding. In the long run, for him, this turned out to be a great background as he moved up the ladder in the manufacturing field.

After boot camp, at the Marine Corps recruit Depot in San Diego, Junior was assigned to the 11th Marine Artillery Battalion. It was stationed at Camp Pendleton California. I was assigned to Baker Company in the 9th Marines. Both the 9th and 11th Marine battalions were part of the 3rd Marine division.

In the summer of 1953 the Third Marine Division prepared to sail. Were we heading to Korea? We did not know. My guess was we were headed to Korea. While we were at sea the Korean Truce we signed. The Korean Peace Treaty said you could replace troops, but not add to the total number already in Korea.

Because of the treaties wording the Marine Corps would first have to pull the First Marine Division out of Korea. Then the Corps could replace the First Division with the Third Division.

That quirk in the Peace Treaty, in my opinion, is why the Third Marine division ended up in "direct support" and was stationed in Japan. My guess about our destination was wrong.

The Eleventh Marines were stationed at Camp Mac Nair. Camp Mac Nair is located between the city of Tokyo and Mount Fuji. The area surrounding the camp was fairly lush, with attractive scenery and a nearby lake.

The Ninth Marines were stationed twice at Camp Fuji. Each time it was for one month of field training. Camp Fuji is roughly 180° north of Camp Mac Nair. The North side of Mount Fuji is very different than the Southside. The ground is mostly volcanic ash, lacking in vegetation and much cooler than the south side.

When you view Mount Fuji it looks just like the pictures you see. It has those smooth lines slopping down its sides from the top; the top is flat and snow-covered. Like I said, it is just like the pictures you see of Mount Fuji, Japan.

I had to use the train from Gotimba to Tokyo once in late 1953 so I could visit Junior at Camp Mac Nair. After Boot Camp, that was the last time that we were able to get together until I was discharged in 1956.

When Junior returned home in January of 1955 it required him to pick up where he left off two years earlier. His wife Marilyn had been living with his parents during the two years he was actively serving in the Marines. There also had been a major change in his family's constellation. He now had a 1½ year old son, his family had expanded.

His old job was still available. The question was, did he want it, or did he want to move on to something else? Questions of where to live, where to work and what changes did he want to make were facing Junior and his family. Junior was aware the decisions could not be put off; he had to hit the ground running.

Things in Minnesota had not changed, but Junior was now two crucial years older. He had two years in the military. He had seen a large portion of the world and his family had expanded.

He had to decide whether he would return to his old job or move in another direction. He opted to further his education and move in a new direction. The one area in which he did not change was in his love and interest in deer hunting.

I remained in the Marine Corps one more year. It was a good year. Camp Horno was a new sub-camp at Camp Pendleton. It was the home for the Marine Corps Test Unit. As I remember it we evaluated atomic bomb effects at Desert Rock, Nevada; the size of fire teams and 'vertical envelopment' (helicopters) at Pendleton.

Later on in Vietnam vertical envelopment became a major method used in combat. Subsequent conflicts also have used it. The Navy Seals more recently, as an example, used it in 2011 when they took out Bin Laden, at that time he was our number one terrorist.

None of us have ever had any regrets about our military years or the loss of several deer hunting seasons. In many respects having served in the military opened new doors for us as we traveled through life. The three of us, Junior, Bob and I knew the military years aided us in our personal growth

The three of us lost two to three years of Minnesota deer hunting by serving in the service; do any of us have any regrets? Absolutely none; and under the same circumstances we would do it again.

When we returned home we all picked up our hunting and fishing interests. Our dedication to our hunting interests is found in the way we have stuck to our long time deer hunting commitment.

How we have helped others join the deer hunting fraternity is an important part of how we live and how we will continue to live. The stories we share with you in this book are because of our love and commitment to hunting and the outdoors.

Chapter 4

THE 1955 MINNESOTA DEER HUNT

I was still in the Marine Corps throughout 1955. Junior had been discharged in January of 1955. That gave him a chance to pick up where he left off in January of 1953.

His dad, Clarence, and three brothers had kept our deer hunting camp at Bigfork going in 1953 and 1954. Junior checked out who would be available to hunt with him in the fall. His two youngest brothers, Leon and Punky, were available and more than happy to go deer hunting with their oldest brother.

For Junior, there was no doubt that they were going back to Bigfork. They would hunt in the area Buck had introduced us to in 1952.

Junior had written to me prior to the 1955 season and told me what their plans were for their hunt. At the time, I was stationed at Camp Pendleton in California. A couple of my Marine buddies and I did some deer hunting in northern California that year. It was the first time that I ever hunted utilizing a "buck law," that is, we could only take a fork horn buck or better. We weren't successful hunting in northern California.

I was anxious to hear how Junior and his brothers did in Minnesota. Junior must have mailed a letter to me first thing Monday morning after their hunt. The three brothers were successful. I received his letter on Wednesday, the day before Thanksgiving.

Camp Pendleton is a large Marine Corps military reservation and is divided into several parts: the main camp, tent camp 1, tent camp 2 and several other sub areas. At that time I was assigned to Camp Horno, home of the newly formed Marine Corps Test Unit, MCTU. Camp Horno is geographically located between Tent Camps 1 and 2.

It was a great place, and just outside our barracks was a very nicely-wooded ravine. The ravine was a haven for the small California black-tail deer.

After I received Junior's letter, telling of the great success they had during their Minnesota deer hunt, I was again ready to go hunting myself.

I suggested to one of my buddies that we walk up the ravine and see if we could harvest a deer. My friend thought it was a good idea. So on Thanksgiving Day 1955, the two of us, with our M-1s, went hunting. We harvested a nice doe.

A few days later with six or so of our friends, we were able to have a venison barbecue on San Clemente Beach. The above is what I was doing in 1955. It has nothing to do with our Bigfork hunting. It was just a highlight based on the success Junior and his brothers had while hunting the Bigfork area in 1955. You might say that their success motivated me to try hunting the area just outside our barracks.

Junior's rendition of their 1955 hunt is a good one. It points out many of the trials and tribulations we all went through in the early years at our deer hunting camp.

Chapter 4
The 1955 Minnesota Deer Hunt
Junior Sjodin

In January of 1955 at the conclusion of my two year enlistment I was discharged by the Marine Corps. In January of 1953 when I joined the Marines I was married and they only accepted married men on a two year reserve enlistment. That didn't break my heart. I was ready to serve and was happy to do so. At that time the Korean conflict appeared to be in a stalemate status. If I had been drafted it would have been for two years, so I was happy for the two year enlistment.

The Marine Corps offered me several good opportunities. The first was the development of my shooting ability. I always enjoyed the shooting sports. In Marine Boot Camp I fired a 228 on the rifle range. It was the highest score in our platoon of approximately 70 Marine Boots.

My 228 score on the rifle range was a good 'expert' score. Later on it offered me several opportunities to participate in rifle matches as a Marine marksman.

I served in the Eleventh Marines, an artillery battalion. The Eleventh Marines were part of the Third Marine Division. The Division in the summer of 1953 sailed to Asia. The Battalion ended up in Camp Mc Nair, Japan. The camp was located near the base of Mt. Fuji, not far from Tokyo. It offered me a chance to see a different culture and a different part of the world.

The year I was stationed at Camp Mc Nair was a great experience for me. At the time I was the artillery batteries clerk and the Captains jeep driver. The officers in our battalion were excellent examples for the men to follow. During that year I had several experiences that highlighted my time in Japan.

With my hunting and fishing background I was curious about the lake that was near our base. I talked to our house boy and he told me about his fishing in the lake. He and I went fishing one day, not really fishing it was actually spearing.

When we got to the lake he let me use his small spear. As I waded through the water I was able to see the fish swimming away from me. They were only the size of a good crappie. As luck would have it I actually speared one.

I handed the fish to my new friend and partner and started fishing again. Later, when I turned around he had the fish half eaten. His comment to me was, "Hey Marine, number one chow." He offered to share the fish with me. To my house boy that fish was a real treat, for me raw fish wasn't going to be part of my Japanese fishing experience.

One day three of my buddies and I decided to climb Mount Fuji. Mount Fuji has an elevation over 12,395 feet, when we started it was at the 3000 foot level. It took hours to accomplish the climb up and back down. All four of us made it up and back and can honestly say, "We did it."

During the fall of 1953, I was playing center on a nine man football team that represented the Eleventh Marine Battalion and Camp Mc Nair. We had a few home games at Camp Mc Nair and several games at other Army and Marine bases. This also was a great experience. I was able to see and tour other parts of Japan.

It was only what they call "flag" football, but the way us Marines went at it, tackle football would be more accurate. The other good part, our team won the championship over all the other military bases in Japan.

Because I came from Anoka County in Minnesota I knew about tornadoes and wind. Over a course of years I had been in one or on the edge of at least five tornadoes. At Camp Mc Nair we did not have tornadoes but during my year there we had two typhoons go through our camp.

Even though I knew about tornadoes and wind, the wind and rain from the typhoons were worse. Our twelve man squad tents were draped over 2"x4" frames, even so they and the canvas held up through the typhoons.

After my two years in the Marine Corps I returned home to my wife Marilyn and my one year old son Chuck. At that time I could go back to my old job or try something new. I decided to do something different.

I hired on at Northern Ordinance as a welding/layout helper. The pay was much better and offered me some chances for advancement. I also entered a vocational school and took a course in welding and metal layout work. Both of these changes proved to be good decisions over the years.

Marilyn found a nice apartment north of Camden in the Minneapolis area. It was a good starter apartment for the two of us and our son Chuck. The apartment served our family for two years.

Later that spring as I was looking ahead to the fall hunt my first priority was a new rifle. I went down to the local hardware store and purchased a Winchester model '94 Lever action 32 special. It was one of those deals where I could put $10 down and $10 a month. I was able to pick up the rifle later on after I completed paying the total cost of $65. Over time my 32 special has served me well. It also turned out to be a good investment.

I chose the 32 caliber rifle over the more popular 30/30. The reason I wanted a 32 special was because of a hunting experience I had with Charlie and his stepdad the second weekend of the 1951 season. Some of their friends were going to make a drive on the last day of the deer season. They wanted Charlie, his stepdad and I along. We made the drive on the NE corner the land where the Anoka County airport is now located. We chased a doe out and as it was jumping over a fence one of the hunters shot it with a 32 Winchester Special, Model '94. I was so impressed I decided that the 32 caliber would be a good choice for my rifle.

By the time the season finally arrived, I was working nights (3-11 pm shift) at Northern Ordinance. The weather report was not good and within several hours it started to snow.

The weather man was predicting blizzard conditions throughout the state. After several hours I went to the shop superintendent, who also was a hunter, and asked if I could leave early. He knew I had a long drive ahead of me and let me check out early and get started heading north.

In this way I was able to pick up my brothers, Leon and Punky. They were living at home between Minneapolis and Anoka on the E. River Rd. That helped because it was on my route to Bigfork.

We had been preparing for this hunting trip all summer and fall. My dad had taken the time to build a rugged sled. It was like the ones the dog teams in Alaska pulled when we lived there. Dad's comment to me was "Boys you can load 1000 pounds on it and go 1000 miles with this sled." In addition to the rope for pulling it had sturdy handle bars on the back. With the handle bars the sled could be pushed as well as pulled.

When I picked my brothers up we loaded our gear in the back seat and trunk of my 1950 Plymouth. The sled was hoisted and put on top of the car. We had chains in the trunk along with canvass and the wood burning stove I made of tin just for our Lean-To-Camp.

On our way up to Bigfork we stopped in Grand Rapids for a bite to eat. Back in those days we always stopped at Mickey's Café. We would have pancakes and eggs or whatever each of us wanted.

By the time the three of us reached Grand Rapids we already had 6 inches of snow on the ground. There was a good crowd going in and out of the café. As we were sitting, eating and enjoying our meal we overheard several people at nearby tables commenting on the "neat sled" that was on top of a car in the parking lot.

We sure felt proud of Dad's creation as we heard the positive comments. As other hunters at the restaurant came out and admired Dad's sled we took the time to tell them about it. The other hunters who looked our sled over said it sure was the "real thing" for our current weather conditions.

By the time we got to Bigfork and the 'minimum maintenance' road leading up to the Smith Farm we had at least 10 inches of snow. We took the time to chain up and were able to make it to the logging road. We could not drive back to our preferred camping spot. There was too much snow on the logging road for us to attempt it, especially at night. We were forced to unload on the road. We were prepared for just such an emergency. We had my dad's newly built sled for transporting our gear to a camp site.

The sled had great handlebars and wood runners for pulling and pushing the sled. We loaded all our gear on the sled and started pushing and pulling the sled east over the logging road. Everything was going great. The runners were sliding over the snow better than expected.

At least the sled worked well for the first 1000 feet. At that point one of the runners collapsed. A collapsed runner was definitely not part of our plan. We had to repair the runner. My brother Leon took a hatchet and cut a curved branch so we could rebuild the collapsed runner on the sled. After we rebuilt the sleds runner we started out again.

That repair lasted 100 feet. So much for the 1000 miles that dad thought his sled would be good for. It was time for a change in our plans. It was getting later, the snow was piling up and it was cold.

We were close to Smith's old potato field. I told the boys, "This is our new camping spot." Right there alongside the logging road we built our lean-to. We cut several poles, tied them together for the frame and covered the frame with our canvas. Under the lean-to we put 12 inches of pine boughs on the ground. The boughs made a fairly comfortable bed for us in the 10° below zero weather. It was now past midnight and time to hit the hay. We wanted to be on our stands fairly early in the morning.

Saturday morning we fired up the wood stove, it turned red-hot in a minute or two. As we were warming up, we got dressed and we were now able to get a big campfire going in front of the lean-to. It had to be at least 10 degrees below zero that night. With the big fire burning and throwing out lots of heat we warmed up rapidly.

It was time to start breakfast. With our two fires going we were ready to start cooking. Soon we found out our food was frozen. Fried eggs were a problem. To solve the problem I peeled the frozen eggs. I set them on the hot frying pan and they gradually thawed out.

Needless to say it took longer to fry the eggs under these conditions than was normal. Frozen eggs will melt. I just don't recommend them as an easy way to prepare a breakfast. With breakfast behind us, it was time to move out and start hunting.

Because of the weather conditions, mostly the snow, we were camping over two miles west of the area I planned for us to hunt. After breakfast we started walking east on the logging road. During the night we received several more inches of snow. Because the snow was light and it was the first big snow storm of the year the going wasn't too bad. It was still a mile walk to the survey line and another mile to the well.

We dropped Leon off at the survey line. He had hunted on the survey line the year before with our dad and knew where to sit. Leon's rifle for our hunt in 1955 was the same Japanese rifle our uncle had brought home after WW II. In 1950, I too, had used that same Jap rifle. I shot my first buck north of Leech Lake with it that year.

After dropping Leon off Punky and I continued heading east for another three fourths mile. At the Tee in the road we took a left and headed for my well stand. This was Punky's first deer hunt. I had to make sure he knew where he could shoot before I left him. I left Punky sitting with his shotgun and slugs on a log just before the well.

From this position he had two major shooting lanes. Once I knew that he was comfortable, at least as comfortable as you could be in 10 degrees below weather, I left him.

I continued past the well and headed west on another logging road. I soon found a large log to sit on and made myself as comfortable as I could in the ten below zero weather. After the long walk to reach my hunting spot I had to open my vest and let the steam out. After a long walk even in cold weather you work up a sweat and need to let your clothes air out a little.

Even though it was really cold it was a great morning in the woods. As I was sitting there chickadees and nuthatches were running up and down the tree trunks looking for whatever food they could find. I had expected to see a ruff grouse but none ever showed up. During the early morning it had quit snowing. In total we had close to a foot of snow. If we had to drag a deer the snow would be perfect.

Because of the snow it was very quiet in the woods. I had been setting there for 30 to 40 minutes and about 8 AM I heard a twig snap. I turned my head just a little and saw a 10 point buck staring at me. I was able to raise my rifle and take a quick shot at the buck.

My shot was low in the front shoulder and went through his liver. He bounded toward me, as he jumped over me and the log I was sitting on, my second shot hit him in the throat. After all the commotion I found myself lying flat on the ground.

Right after my second shot his momentum carried him several feet. He fell only a few feet from where I was laying. He was a big whitetail buck. When we got home my uncle estimated his field dressed weight at 260 pounds.

Now that I had my first Bigfork buck, a nice one at that, the work would really start. Field dressing him was the first job. My youngest brother Punky and I started the second job, the two mile drag back to our camp.

As we were dragging my buck on the logging road we startled a buck fawn. I took a quick 'hip shot' and broke the deer's back. That little deer let out the loudest 'blatting' I ever heard coming from a wounded animal. I will never do a back shot again.

Now we really had our hands full. The buck fawn was easy to drag. But when you combined that with the big buck we had our hands full. After many breaks and an hour or more we finally made it to the survey line.

We left the two deer on the logging road and walked down the survey line to check on Leon. Leon told us he had taken a shot at a deer. When he had checked it out he found some hair on the snow but no blood trail. He went back to where he was sitting and continued watching the survey line. He was hoping the deer would return.

Because Punky and I were pooped from dragging the two deer, I shot, I sent Leon back to camp to get us some food. I had told Leon that we would see if we could find his deer.

I had Punky follow the tracks of the deer Leon had shot at. He must have only gone about 100 yards when he yelled back, "I found it." I yelled, "Shoot it". He yelled back "But it's blinking its eyes at me". I again yelled back, "Shoot the damn thing". I heard the bang, now our licenses were filled.

By midday on the opening day of the 1955 deer season we were filled. The short drag of Leon's deer to the logging road and then the mile to the minimum maintenance road with all three deer was still ahead of us. As I said before the work starts after you harvest the animals.

After field dressing Leon's doe we dragged the deer up to the logging road. Leon returned shortly with our lunch and we all took a well-deserved short break. After lunch we again were dragging deer down the logging road toward camp. As we dragged the deer we kept shedding our clothing. We were down to our shirtsleeves when we finally arrived at our camp.

As we were dragging our deer we ran into a couple of other hunters. They had walked by our lean-to camp and were amazed that we had used it for sleeping in 10 degree below weather. They invited us to use their heated fish house to warm up and dry our sweaty clothes. We definitely took them up on their offer.

One of the other hunters was named Bulduc. I had met him back in 1952. Because he worked at the Lakeville Post Office we started calling his group the Post Office Party. His son's still hunt in an area alongside ours and are using a cabin they built on 40 acres they purchased years ago. Because of this 10 below zero snowy winter experience and our lean-tos in 1952 and 1955 they started calling us "The Lean-To-Boys."

After warming up and drying off we packed our gear so we would be ready to go in the morning. By that time it was getting late and we spent one more night in our lean-to in 10 degrees below zero weather. The next morning we broke camp and headed for home.

One thing I know; we did not return home with the broken down "1000 mile" sled that was only good for 1000 feet. To this day I do not remember what we did with the sled.

When I got home there was still two jobs remaining. The first was to crank off a letter to Charlie and second we had three deer to butcher. The beauty was we didn't have to do it in 10 degrees below zero weather.

Chapter 5

DEER HUNTING IN 1956 THE FIRST WEEKEND

Charlie Turnbull

Things were looking good for my first hunt since my discharge from the Marine Corps. This was my first year back hunting with the Lean-To-Boys. Clarence, Junior, Punky and I made the trip the first weekend. This was another year similar to 1952; the temperature was moderate and we had no snow.

Even though the weather was similar to 1952, the deer hunting was much slower. In 1952, we saw a lot of deer. We were not seeing a lot of activity and we did not harvest any deer on the opening day.

The second day also started out very slow. At noon, we decided to make a drive to the survey line. The starting point would be about three-fourths of a mile east of the survey line.

When the drive started, Clarence and I were the drivers. Junior was stationed on the survey line and Punky was walking the logging road. The plan was for me to make lots of noise by banging on trees and doing a lot of yelling. We hoped that lots of noise would get the deer moving.

Clarence would be to my left, but he would hang back a little just in case any deer tried to sneak around me and out to the south. We did not want to miss any. The drive started with me yelling and banging on trees; my goal was to make a lot of noise.

About half way through the drive, Clarence got a shot and put down a nice eight-point buck. I walked back towards my left and found him and his deer. When I knew Clarence had everything under control, I continued the drive. As I was approaching the survey line, I heard Junior's shot. When I reached the survey line, I found that Junior had harvested a nice doe.

After the drive, Clarence said the buck didn't even know he was coming. The deer was standing and was only paying attention to the noise and racket I was making on the drive. Clarence's strategy of holding back on the drive really paid off.

Although we didn't do well on Saturday, we did come up with two deer on Sunday. By the time we were through dragging the deer out of the woods, it was getting late in the day.

1956 was a good year, but not an outstanding year for deer hunting. It was the start of a six-year period of time when my deer hunting would be limited. I could only devote the time from Friday evening through Sunday afternoon. My new family status, studies at the University of Minnesota, and part-time work demanded my attention during the week.

Clarence, Punky and Junior were not planning on going to Bigfork for the second weekend. I made plans with our friend Pete to go hunting the second weekend. My boss, Lee, asked if he and his friend could join us. I invited them to join us up at Bigfork.

Pete is another friend from our high school and farming days. In high school, he was one year behind us. Pete's folks owned a farm a mile east of our family farm. Junior, Pete and I had done a fair amount of pheasant and duck hunting in the fields and ponds throughout the Constance area. In 1951, Pete hunted with us in southern Minnesota. The three of us had a long history of hunting together. For some reason, he missed the deer hunt we had "up north" in 1952.

Pete had an older brother who had been a Marine in Korea. His brother was serving in Korea when he became a Marine, Killed in

Action. He had been a combat Marine with the First Marine Division when it invaded North Korea in the fall of 1950.

Pete has always identified himself with the Marine Corps. I always had the feeling that Pete's older brother was a hero to him. At one time I thought he would be joining the Corps at the same time Junior and I did.

He waited until the fall of 1953. When he finally did enlist in the Corps, he waived his exemption as a sole surviving son. At that time Junior and I were overseas with the Third Marine Division.

In the fall of 1956, Pete requested an early release from the Corps. In that way he could enter Hamline University in St. Paul, Minnesota. The Marine Corps granted his request. That also opened the door for some hunting that fall.

When Pete was granted his early out he was not eligible to receive a good conduct medal. Pete has always said he should have been given the Good Conduct Medal anyway.

Pete did receive the China Service Medal because of his time in a maneuver in the China seas area in 1954. It came after he was discharged.

In the Marine Corps, you have to complete three years of service to be eligible to receive the Good Conduct Medal. Pete was two months short of the required time. Rules in the Marine Corps do not bend easily, not even for Pete. Of all our friends who served in the Corps, he is the most dedicated. Everybody who has ever been associated with him learns about the Marine Corps.

The Second Week End
Pete Wojciechowski

I read above what Charlie said about my brother and my receiving the China Service Medal. This is what happened with me and my brother and the Corps in 1954.

I was officially notified by the Marine Corps that I would be the escort for my brother Larry when they dug him up at Yudam-ni, North Korea. The trip in December of 1954, from Japan to Minnesota, was via Midway Island, Hawaii, San Francisco and on to Minnesota. We arrived home on Christmas Eve 1954. Larry was buried at the National Cemetery at Fort Snelling. It was a personal honor for me to be able to escort my brother home from Korea.

My next orders sent me back via San Francisco, Hawaii, Wake Island to Yokosuka and on to China. We were on board a naval ship that had some mission there, one where we blew up something. It garnered us the China Service Medal.

I got out of the Corps in August and this was my first hunt in three years. I was a first year student at Hamline University and could only devote one weekend to deer hunting.

When the hunting season in 1956 started I did not go with Charlie and Junior the first weekend. The second week end fit me better.

Charlie and I ventured up to Bigfork the second weekend. I volunteered to drive my 1939 Studebaker. I called it "the Grey Goose." With the Grey Goose we were able to get good gas mileage. We did have to live with the "Gooses" broken shock absorbers.

It was late on Friday when we took off for Bigfork. It was a long drive in the dark. We reached the logging road in good shape and headed down the logging road to the proposed camp site.

All we had to do was make sure the four logs crossing the creek were in their proper place. We reached the creek and I stopped. My "self-appointed" guide, Charlie, got out checking the log rails I was to drive on to cross the creek.

This was supposed to be a no-brainer. There were four logs two for each set of tires on the right and left side of the Grey Goose.

To test the logs he kicked them. Charlie reported that they were frozen in place. We would have no problem crossing the creek tonight in the dark. He reassured me we can drive over them.

Ok, I said, and started driving across on the two sets of parallel logs. I was taking it easy and the front end reached the far side. The rear tires were over 50 percent of the way across when the so called 'frozen in place' logs did a special version of the splits.

The rear end of my Studebaker, the "Grey Goose," settled nicely onto the two sets of parallel logs. The front end was on solid ground and the rear end was hanging over the creek, supported by the not so frozen in the ground, split apart but parallel logs. The tires were hung up in outer space with little chance for the traction they deserved.

My scout and I slept in the not so level car that night. Tomorrow would be another day.

The next day we had great opportunities to rehash our Marine Corps basic profane vocabulary. Each time we moved forward we made some progress, but it was not a labor of love.

We jacked the Goose's rear end up time after time. In our frustration we cussed some more. Eventually the rear end made it to the same solid ground as the front end.

We had a choice to make. Use the logs on a return trip or fill in the creek bed so we could drive over the debris. We could tie the logs together but if they did the splits we had a half days work ahead of us. I opted to fill in the creek bed. We laid logs crossways in the creek bed. We did the same with brush, sticks and even more logs until we felt comfortable with the creek beds stability.

I was finally ready to try to get the Grey Goose on the safe side of the creek. I revved the Gooses engine, you might say, I "goosed" it, and took off for the safe side. I started across, I bounced, I got tossed around but I made it. The Grey Goose was now on solid ground where the tires had the traction they deserved.

If we had tied the two logs together we probably would've been successful in crossing the creek. It was finally time to think about hunting. The good thing about the whole situation was the weather. It was a fairly mild winter and we were not fighting the cold.

Charlie's boss, where he worked, and his friend joined us for the hunt that weekend. We spent the morning jacking up the Grey Goose. They did the hunting. Later in the morning we joined them and decided to make the same basic drive the Lean-To-Boys did the week before. Just like them, if we were going to be successful we needed to get the deer moving.

Charlie and I agreed to be the drivers. The other two were put on stands. We were successful in driving a doe to the stander on the survey line. He was successful in harvesting that doe. The way it worked out it was the only deer we saw that weekend.

The hunting that weekend was slow. Because of all the racket and activity we were involved in, it is no wonder the deer were scarce. The woods were nice to look at but I don't think there were any deer in the immediate area. Except the one we had to go and find. There is always next year. It has to be better.

Chapter 6

TOO MUCH SNOW IN '57

Charlie Turnbull

We were anticipating having an especially good hunt in 1957. The weather was not too cold, and snow was predicted. As we drove north on Friday it was even snowing. Snow the day before the opening of the season was a very good omen.

We wanted snow and we were having our wishes fulfilled. By the time we settled in for the night, we had over 8 inches of snow. During the night, it continued to snow, and by morning we had close to a foot of new snow.

As we were looking out of our tent, the snow was a welcome sight. After a reasonably quick breakfast, we were ready to go out and start hunting.

When we were out in the open, the snow did not look as good as we first thought. As we looked into the woods and brush it became apparent that we could not see over ten to fifteen feet in the woods.

The snow on the ground was perfect. The snow hanging on every branch, limb, twig, leaf and or piece of grass was at least two inches deep. The temperature was close to 32 degrees and the snow was wet and sticky. By the time you walked twenty five yards, you were wet and well on your way to being a miserable hunter.

Finding a deer or even tracks was not happening. Apparently, the deer were bedded down and not moving. Even if they were moving, with the visibility at 10 to 15 feet we would not get an opportunity to take a shot.

We definitely had the snow we had wanted, and had been so happy for, on Friday. On Saturday, things looked a whole lot different.

The question was, what do we do now? Because of the snow, the deer were not moving; we had to get them moving. We organized a drive and went in after the deer.

The drive was somewhat successful; a buck was driven out and passed one of the standers. As it crossed the logging road, the buck, was leaping for the cover of the pines on the other side. The man on the stand took a quick shot and missed. It was the best opportunity we had that weekend.

The people who did the driving were soaked to their skin. Nobody was ready to try another drive that day.

We ended up with a deer count of zero for that season's first weekend. Maybe something was learned from the experiences with the excess snow we had in 1957. Have rain gear available was one and another was not to start out overly optimistic. It soon can become a big letdown.

If the same conditions were to happen now, decades later, we would handle it a lot better. In 1957, we did not use stands as a major part of our method for deer hunting. Now we do.

Because of the way we now hunt deer, we would drive to our stands. We would brush them off, take a seat, start the "buddy heater" and wait the deer out. The deer eventually do (or will) move around; patience is the key factor in waiting them out.

The second weekend, we ended up on the iron range at Aurora, Minnesota. Punky, Wilson and I went to the McGrath game preserve that had been opened up for deer hunting that year. We wanted to see if that was better. Evidently, it had been very good on the opening weekend.

When we arrived, the snow-covered woods looked like a doctor's chart of the human blood system. Small arteries and veins were joining larger one, and the larger ones were connected to an even larger one.

The woods were full of the blood-red paths. What we saw was very similar to the chart described above. Deer had been dragged out of the woods with one path leading to and joining another, and so on until the final path looked like a bloody four-lane highway.

McGrath must have been fabulous the first weekend. The old sign and blood trails were evidence of the success hunters had earlier in the season.

Four days later we did not see any deer or fresh sign. The first weekend must have been a real shooting fray. On Thursday after our arrival, we could not find even one fresh track.

At noon, we regrouped for lunch and decided to pack up and head to the Aurora area. The Aurora area was new to all of us, so we all went in different directions. In my wandering around the area, I found an area that looked promising.

The snow was still falling, it was deep, and there were fresh tracks and deer beds in the area. As I moved off a small rise and into a more wooded area, I came upon 10 to 12 even fresher deer beds.

It was snowing, and the beds were clear of snow. I must have scared them off. As I was surveying the situation and looking around, I saw a deer. He must not have heard the others leave. As luck would have it, I did harvest the deer. It was the only deer five of us saw that weekend.

1957 was finally over; it was not the season we dreamed about at the beginning. Now it was time to look forward and start the planning needed for the 1958 season.

Chapter 7

MY FIRST BIG WHITETAIL

Charlie Turnbull

1958 was a good year for our party at the Lean-To-Boys' camp. It was a year when the three of us, Junior, Pete and I, were in the camp and we all were Marine veterans.

Even though we had some snow, the weather was fairly mild. That fall, there had been quite a bit of rain. When it rained excessively, the road into our camping area became soggy and impassable. This was one of those years.

This was a major problem. As soon as we turned off the minimum maintenance road, we had trouble. As we started driving down the logging road to our camp, we hit an extended series of mud holes.

The mud holes had deep ruts in them caused by another hunting party. That party owned a surplus military Dodge Power Wagon, a vehicle that could handle the problems the mud holes presented. Without four-wheel-drive, we could not make it through the deeply-rutted mud holes.

We had to park our car on the "minimum maintenance road." That forced us to backpack our gear to camp. The distance between our car and our campsite was over a mile. Back then, we were still in good enough shape to handle the work that was needed. I think the training the three of us had received in the Corps was still helping us.

Our campsite was at the same location that we used in 1952. It was a good starting point. We were close to the area we planned to hunt. On cold days, a short walk was better than a long one.

On cold days, it was important not to work up a sweat. If you do, a sweat works against your staying warm on a stand. The evaporation from the sweat has that "damn cooling effect." The weather can cool your body. You don't have to help it.

Opening morning, I was using Junior's rifle, a Winchester 32 special. At that time, it was equipped with Winchester's standard open sight. We had traded our rifles because he was going to hunt west of camp on the survey line. It would be better if he had my Remington 300 Savage with its scope sight.

My plan was to hunt a smaller opening in the woods east of our camp. At the most, I would probably be shooting no more than 60 to 70 yards. At the survey line, Junior might be shooting as far as 200 yards. It was a good trade for our purposes.

I hiked through the 8 inches of snow to the place I had picked out to hunt. It was a small clearing on the west side of a North/South logging road. I did not have a stand to sit on as I had opted to find a stump or else sit on the ground. After an hour I grew tired of sitting on the ground. In addition I was starting to get wet and cold from the melting snow. It was time to take a hike.

The wet snow cushioned the woods, and walking in the grassy areas was exceedingly quiet. I started walking north along the east edge of the clearing. As I approached the north end of the clearing, I noticed that there was more swale grass and fewer trees to my right. I only traveled a short distance when I saw three deer to my right front. They were approximately 60 yards away. I took aim at the doe and shot. My shot had the same effect for the three deer as the starting gun at a swim or track meet. The deer were off and running before I could chamber another round in the rifle.

I walked through the snow and wet swale grass to where the deer had been standing. There was no blood or hair. I followed the trail through the snow for several hundred yards. Still there was no evidence that I had hit the deer. Then I walked out to the North/South Logging Road. As I walked, I came across a set of fresh deer tracks heading east into the woods.

It was a nice day and the snow had started to melt. Because of the melting, my trousers had become wet. Walking and following the deer track was the best way to warm up and dry off.

Following the deer tracks was a good learning experience for me. The tracks headed southeast and then turned south. I followed the deer across a narrow ridge through a large swampy area. I was fairly sure the tracks leading south were headed toward an area east of a caved-in trapper's cabin. If I was right, I now knew another way to get to the area on the south side of the swamp.

Once the deer crossed the swamp, the deer trail started up and onto a finger of land. In doing so, the deer also crossed a logging road. I wasn't sure, but I felt it was the logging road heading east from the dilapidated cabin.

After reaching the logging road, I lost the deer track I had been following. The deer I was following had come to an area where several deer had made multiple tracks.

As I was walking west on the logging road, a deer leaped across it. It was too far away and too quick for me to get a shot.

The number of deer tracks had literally multiplied in the short distance I had traveled. To my left, there appeared to be more deer tracks. There were fewer trees to my left, so I walked over to investigate. Because of the deer I had seen and the number of tracks in the area, I felt that things were looking up.

I just walked a few yards south when I heard the thumping of a running deer. It was not running away from me. It was running in an oblique angle toward me. As the deer was running past me, I was able to take a shot. Again I missed.

She kept running approximately 25 yards and came to an abrupt stop. Again, I had a standing shot at about 25 yards. I missed again. By this time, I was starting to question what was going on. After I took that second shot, I walked over to where she had been standing. I was looking for blood, hair or any indication that I had hit that doe.

I doubt if I stood in her tracks more than a minute or two. It was then that I saw the head of a buck coming from behind several small evergreen trees. The buck's head and nose were close to the ground. Even though I had just shot twice, it appeared that the buck was not concerned, nor was he aware, that I was in the area.

As the deer came around the trees, he lifted his head high. He was walking straight toward me. Not only was he walking straight toward me. He was less than 20 feet away. I lifted the rifle and took a shot. He dropped right at my feet. This time I had my deer, a very nice eight pointer.

You hear stories about the "rut" and its effect on bucks. When the bucks are chasing does that are in heat, they do things that appear dumb to us. The buck that I had just harvested was a good example of their actions during the rutting season. It boils down to this; when a buck is trying to do his job, to keep the species going, his mind is on his job, not his safety.

I knew I had a big buck. When I weighed him five days later, he hit 204 pounds field dressed. At that time, he was the biggest deer I had ever harvested.

What a relief. I had finally been able to down a deer that morning. Now I had to field dress the buck and figure out which way to drag him to camp. The field dressing was a pleasure.

It did not take me long to figure out my need for help in dragging him back to camp. The exact route I should take was definitely a question. I could head west and hope the logging road was the one I thought it was; or I could backtrack to the logging road where I had started.

If for some reason I were to get lost, I might not be able to find my downed deer. The snow was melting rapidly. In the woods, the melting was much slower. For that reason, I opted to back track the deer trail back to the other logging road.

When I reached the other logging road I headed south, then east to our camp. Pete and Junior were in camp when I got there. They had come in for lunch. I briefed them about my experiences that morning.

Shortly after lunch, we all headed out from camp in the direction of my deer. When we got to the tee in the logging road, I had them go south. By going south, they would walk out to the collapsed trapper's cabin. I went north, found my tracks, and back tracked them to my deer.

Even though the snow had continued to melt, there was still enough in the woods to follow. Finding the buck was not a problem. The plan was for me to call after I found the deer.

When I called, they returned my call. They had already started walking east and were already close, only a short distance west of me by that time. I had been right. The logging road I was on was the one that led to and from the rundown cabin.

Once the three of us were together, we knew the way to camp and were aware of the long drag ahead of us. On the way back to camp, two would pull the deer; the other one would take a break.

Even though I had seen at least seven or eight deer on opening day, Pete and Junior had not seen any. At least none they could shoot. This is one area that hunting and fishing have in common. Sometimes one person sees most of the game. In fishing, many times one fisherman catches the most fish. The next time around the roles reverse.

On Sunday, we filled Pete and Junior's deer tags. I went back to the area where the rundown cabin was located. I shot a fawn first thing in the morning. It was in the same general area where I shot the buck the day before. I was sitting on a log near the cabin when the fawn came into the clearing. With my own rifle, he was easy pickings. I didn't need any help dragging the fawn back to camp.

Junior shot a big doe at midday. When Junior harvested that doe he was sitting on his "well stand." I had walked out with Junior to his stand, in that way, I could make a drive for him. I left him and worked my way around on the logging roads so that I was north of where he was sitting.

I made a one-man drive to where he was stationed at the "well stand." A big doe moved out ahead of me heading in Junior's direction. The doe crossed the logging road close to Junior. As I was working my way through the woods, I heard the crack of his rifle. When I reached the logging road, Junior was already in the process of field dressing the doe. It was a great way to end the hunt.

When all was said and done, Junior and I discussed my misses with his 32 special. The rifle was sighted in properly. The fault for missing was mine. The open sight has to be used properly. The front bead of the rifle, when sighted properly, has to be seated in the rounded bottom of the "V" back part of the sight. If the front bead sits high in the "V," the barrel it is more than likely pointing up and you are shooting over your target. I believe that is why I missed those first two does. I shot over them. When I downed the buck I hit him high in the neck. If he had not been coming directly toward me, with his head up, I might have shot over his back, too.

The bottom line is, if you're not familiar with the rifle and its sighting demands, taking it out hunting is a poor plan. Another lesson learned. A peep sight automatically keeps your front bead when sighted through the peep hole in its proper placement. A scope automatically does the same for the shooter. My preference has always been the use of a scope.

Yes, 1958 was a good year for hunting. We had filled our three tags in a day and a half. Even though we had snow, the weather turned out to be very livable. 1958 turned out to be a predecessor to a six-year span of good hunting.

Chapter 8

ONE COLD YEAR

Doug started hunting with the Lean-To-Boys in 1959. He couldn't have started with us any year that was colder than 1959. Doug was originally from North Dakota. He was used to the cold and the blustery winds that North Dakota had to offer.

Doug was Junior's neighbor and really was looking forward to our hunt that year. He hunted with us for about 10 years. He was a good hunter but did not like the big woods. He was used to the flat plains of North Dakota. Later on when he retired, he returned to his roots in North Dakota.

Before his retirement, Doug went on to work at Ray Go Manufacturing. Junior had hired him because of his good work attitude, mechanical skills and his ability to follow through on a job.

Chapter 8
One Cold Year
Doug Mitchell

Talk about cold, we had it the first weekend of the 1959 deer hunting season. It never was warmer than 10 degrees below zero even at mid-day.

That first morning it must have been more than 15 degrees below zero. At mid-afternoon, when the sun hit the 45 degree angle in the West the dropping temperature was hard to live with. In Minnesota when it's cold and the temperature is dropping it chills you to the bone. That's the way it was during the 1959 deer season.

The cold was not a one-day drop in the temperature. It was there when we arrived at camp on Friday. It was there when we left on Sunday afternoon. The cold spell lasted way past the nine day season. By the second weekend it was even colder.

The weather predictions had been correct. They had predicted very cold weather in November. We had listened to the predictions and took them to heart. Junior and I decided to use one of our fish houses for our shelter that first weekend. The fish house was approximately 6 feet x 8 feet. We were able to carry it on one of our two wheeled trailers. It was just big enough for us to install four bunks.

We even figured out how to cook in the fish house. By having one bunk on hinges we could lift it out of the way and set up our cooking stove. It was crowded but it worked.

We also had a small heater to take the chill off. The fish house arrangement worked fairly well. Without it we would have been in trouble.

Four hunters cramped into a small space did not leave a lot of elbow room. The one thing the fish house did offer was shelter. We could keep it warm and when we needed to it allowed us to get out of the cold weather.

We reached Bigfork late on Friday afternoon. We could only drive as far as the creek. We had hoped to be able to drive the other mile to our usual campsite. Because of the snow and potential for more snow we chose to set camp up at the creek. The creek was close enough. We could reach our stands and the areas we wanted to hunt from that location.

On most hunts we would stay up till eight or 8:30 PM. Not in 1959, we were tired from our trudging through the snow and our efforts to stay warm. We were in our bunks and sleeping by 7 PM. In the morning about 5 AM we started making the adjustments to our bunks so we could make breakfast.

Saturday morning we headed out to our selected areas or the stand we were planning to use for hunting that day. Clarence wandered out to the rock stand. The rock stand and the area around the stand was one of our better areas for hunting.

Clarence had been moseying around the big rocks near the stand when he spotted a group of five or six deer. Most of them started moving away from Clarence. A spike buck was on the other side of a clump of brush, Clarence thought the buck was playing hide and seek.

If in fact the buck was using the brush as his way to hide from Clarence, it did not work. Clarence was able to get a good shot and harvested the spike buck. It was a good start on a bitterly cold day in the Bigfork woods.

Junior, Clarence and Charlie had the privilege of dragging the deer the mile and a half to our camp. There was snow on the ground so dragging the deer was easier than other times when we had to drag them on dry ground.

I was still standing on my stump at mid-day when they came by me dragging the spike buck. I declined to join them for lunch back at camp.

I really thought Clarence's buck looked real good. I did not want to be in camp and miss an opportunity to get a deer by being off my stand. They did ask if I had seen anything that morning. I told them no, but one had crossed through the grass area west of me before I arrived there in the morning.

I felt the deer were using the tall grass as a place to cross the logging road. I could see the area clearly from my stump.

Several hours later, Charlie stopped by. He was on his way to hunt the area northeast of my stump stand. By the time Charlie arrived and stopped by I had been standing on the stump for seven hours. I knew I had to stick it out. I truly expected that a deer would use the trail some time during the day.

Two hours later, about 4:30 PM, my patience was rewarded. I spotted a doe working her way through the tall grass west of me.

She was on the same trail where I had seen deer tracks early that morning. I was able to get a good clean shot at the doe. We now had two deer for our efforts that first day of the 1959 season.

I had stood on that stump for over nine hours on one of the coldest hunting days of my life. Somehow I must have been dressed warm enough to with-stand the early morning cold and the chill you receive as the temperature dropped in the late afternoon. To me it was worth it, harvesting a deer on my first hunt with the Lean-To-Boys was important to me.

The stump and I, the one on which I had been standing, had almost grown together. During that nine hour period of time I never sat down. In my years of deer hunting with the Lean-To-Boys I never set any records with the deer I shot.

I believe I do have the record for the "longest and coldest" time standing on a stump. I didn't freeze to death, but I want to tell you our hunt was during "one cold year."

Chapter 9

ROMANTIC IDEAS VERSUS COLD REALITY

Several of us hunted both weekends of the 1959 season. The first weekend there were four of us, harvesting two deer. Clarence and Doug were successful, Clarence shooting a spike buck and Doug getting a nice doe. Needless to say, Junior and I were deer-less!

Before I left to go hunting that first weekend, I told my wife, Marlene, that she could go the next weekend. In addition to Junior, Marlene, our foster son, Don and me, Clarence at the last minute decided to go with us.

This was Marlene's first deer hunt "up north." To say the least, it was a real hunting experience. Marlene is a good story teller. Her rendition of that weekend's hunt is best told in her own words.

Chapter 9
Marlene Turnbull
"Romantic Ideas versus Cold Reality"

Charlie and I married July 21, 1956. For six months prior to "the hunt" I listened to the "guys" talking about the preparations for Bigfork and six months after the hunt I listened to their scenarios of the past hunt. The deer season coming up in the fall of 1959 would be the fourth since we were married.

Each year I bugged my husband about going with him, AFTER ALL, I had listened to all the stories. The answer was always NO, "it was only a men's camp." My co-worker Kay at the bookstore regaled me with her deer hunting stories; she always hunted with the men! There were angry tears shed; undoubtedly I wanted him to feel guilty.

I always tell people our wedding vows were hunting, fishing and then Marlene. I knew, even before we married that deer hunting and the comrade he shared with the "Lean-To-Boys" was something really special. I wanted to be part of that group.

During our first three years of marriage I kept nagging and shedding tears. In 1959 he put me off by saying, "If I don't get a deer the first weekend, you can come with me the second weekend." I was really elated when he left.

The next day I needed to go to Hugh's Corner Grocery and Hardware Store in Lexington. I had worked there and knew everyone. I was in the hardware store and told Reiney Johnson that I was going DEER HUNTING, if Charlie didn't get one that weekend. Reiny asked me if I had a license (they sold them at the store) and I said no. He explained, "You have to get one today because this is the last day and we cannot issue a license after today." I bought one right on the spot!

I was "fit to be tied;" I could have lost out on my first deer hunt because I was unaware of the rules. Had Charlie just "neglected" to inform me? But I was prepared! He returned home on Sunday evening and told me that Clarence and Doug each got a deer. Junior and he did not and they would be going back the next weekend. I was REALLY EXCITED; I was going to Bigfork! His first question to me was; "Do you have a license?" I proudly showed it to him.

Now the question was what is needed for this coming trip. That first weekend had been very cold that season in northern Minnesota. The rest of the week was no better, the temperature hovered around zero and on Friday it dropped to a minus 20 degrees below zero. I packed my down flight suit (bought when I lived in South Dakota) and my "bunny boots" and heavy gloves.

We needed two auto-mobiles. Clarence volunteered Punky's convertible. Punky had joined the Marines, so it was available. Convertibles leak cold air and are not really recommended for Minnesota winter driving. Punky's was no different and it was almost impossible to stay warm in 20 to 30 degree below zero weather. The second automobile was our 1958 Ford station wagon. It had recently been hit and the back window had popped out.

We could not afford to fix it. Charlie was going to school at the U of M and we were living on the GI Bill checks and his part time janitorial job at DeVac Window Co. But, Charlie was resourceful and covered the window with plastic and secured it with duct tape. It too leaked and we had the heater on full blast. About two thirds of the way to Bigfork the heater died. We were off to a "cool" start; but in good "Marine Corps" fashion we charged ahead.

No matter, I was on my way to Bigfork to hunt deer and I was as DETERMINED as any Marine, there was no turning back. I had finally broken through the "glass ceiling!" I was with my husband and some of the Lean-To-Boys. It was my chance to win acceptance as a hunter.

It was truly cold that Friday evening; we had left home after 6:00 PM and when we arrived at Bigfork at 2:00 AM we were tired and cold; it had dropped to minus 30 degrees below zero. The first item on the agenda was heat and we built a roaring fire and we were able to enjoy the frigid morning with a full moon and thousands of stars. Our sleeping accommodations were not well thought out. With our heater gone, sleeping or trying to rest in the cars was almost impossible.

There wasn't a cabin, tent or lean-to for shelter. Sleeping in our station wagon with sleeping bags and blankets was the plan. Staying warm became the plan, but it was next to impossible. Finally morning arrived at 5:00 AM. We gathered wood, got a roaring fire going again, had a bite to eat and headed out to our stands.

Even though Clarence, 'the old man' as Junior called him, had harvested a deer the first weekend he joined us on this cool adventure. He chose the logging road heading south along the creek to find a place to hunt.

The rest of us headed east along another logging road. Junior found a place to the south. Next, Charlie placed our foster son Don, and myself on our stands, and told us to watch for deer crossing the logging trail. Charlie continued walking to find a stand. He walked as far as an old abandoned car, where the road and a survey line crossed.

I was now sitting on a stand, hunting deer for hours and TRYING TO STAY WARM in the -30 degree weather. I know Charlie calls this deer hunting; I call it freezing and I did not have to hunt for it!

After several hours I decided to head back to our camp at the creek, chop wood, and build a fire. Growing up on the South Dakota plains, I knew how to chop wood and build fires.

I got Don and we walked back through the crisp sparkling snow. We warmed up by gathering and chopping wood. Soon we had a roaring fire going and we were enjoying the warmth.

By mid-afternoon, Charlie entered camp and was happy to see the fire! He said he had seen one doe but was unable to take a shot. That was encouraging. He asked how our deer hunting went for us. I explained, what he called deer hunting was really "freeze-sitting;" there was no hunting about it!

This day did not have any relationship to the Lean-To-Boys glorified stories or my concept of hunting. After all, I was a girl raised in South Dakota I had hunted pheasants with my Dad; I knew something about hunting.

I walked the railroad tracks with Daddy; the pheasants would fly up and my Dad would shoot them and we would take them home for dinner. After being raised in "Pheasant Country" It would take a long time to get used to Minnesota Freezer Hunting.

I told Charlie it was so nice sitting by the fire, but my feet were starting to get cold and had not been moving around. I decided to take off my boots but that was a mistake. My socks froze to my feet. Charlie laughed, but I didn't think it was funny, but shortly they defrosted. I dried out my bunny boots and put on dry socks; I was finally warm and comfortable. The relaxed atmosphere did not last.

It was now after 4 PM, the shadows were growing longer and dusk would soon be upon us. Then Junior came rushing into camp. He asked if we had seen or heard from his dad, Clarence. We said we had not seen or heard anything. Junior said he had heard some yelling in the woods and it was coming from across the creek. Junior's stand was on the survey line directly across from the area where he had heard yelling. Because of the time of day we were very concerned. Junior, Charlie and Don immediately headed south, the direction Clarence had taken in the morning.

They found Clarence lying under a large evergreen tree. He was conscious, but cold and severely injured. He told them he had fallen out of the tree; Clarence had a reputation for climbing trees and sitting on a branch watching for deer. This time he evidently fell asleep and lost his balance. Junior sent Don back for the toboggan. Don told me that Clarence had fallen from a tree and was severely injured. He told me that I should drive into Bigfork and have an ambulance follow me back to camp.

Even though I was anxious and tense, I drove carefully into town and got an ambulance. They followed me to our camp. Luckily, by that time the guys had arrived in camp with Clarence on the toboggan.

At this time we had the right people telling us what to do, basically stay out of their way. Charlie and Junior told me how painful it was for Clarence when they towed him back to camp, every little bump the pain would shoot through him. We could only pray and hope that Clarence would come out of this in good shape.

The ambulance crew told them when to lift and they got Clarence secured in the ambulance. They told us that Clarence's injuries were not life threatening and from what the EMTs could determine he had a severe back injury. The hospital in Grand

Rapids had the proper equipment to treat Clarence, so that became their destination. They told us they were taking him to the Grand Rapids Hospital.

We were done hunting for the year and still had a long drive home. Junior followed the ambulance. The rest us decided what needed to be done; we packed up our gear to head home. We were cold, hungry and tired. We stopped in Bigfork for dinner and hot coffee then drove to Grand Rapids to check on Clarence. We found that he had a compression fracture, was resting and would need to stay at the hospital a few days, so we all headed home.

Charlie was tired and from his history of falling asleep when driving, I insisted on driving. Soon the windows started frosting up. I tried to wipe a spot in the window with my glove and I dropped it.

Then I turned on the defroster. The heater died on the way up north so I was stuck with cold air from the defroster. I did not want to wake Charlie so I kept moving forward with my one gloved hand. You think it is tough being a Marine, try being a Marine's wife!

Needless to say, as a fairly rational woman, I made a meaningful decision to stop hunting Bigfork. Now I hunt our property near the Norseland Woods in Nicollet County. We built a Hunting Shack and I established the "Women's Hunt." Junior's wife Marilyn, myself, our daughters Char, Mary and Terry and some of the wives of the second generation Lean-To-Boys of Bigfork were the founders of the Camp.

The only male allowed was Charlie; he cooked, brought us sandwiches to our stands, and outfitted us with Coleman catalytic heaters. As time evolved our daughters and their friends went off to college. The young wives were raising families and our female population dropped. Now males are allowed in our camp.

Charlie's notes: Clarence's injuries were treated by the Grand Rapids Hospitals staff. The x-rays confirmed that he had a compression fracture in his spinal column. He remained in the hospital for several days before returning home. He was able to return to work and go on living his life.

He rarely complained of a sore back. But, I would bet he did have back pain from time to time.

He said, because of the compression fracture he was 1 inch shorter. Clarence continued to hunt with the Lean-To-Boys for three or four more years.

Chapter 10

CREATION OF A "SWAMP BUGGY"

Junior is a welder by training and trade. He is a community resource. He was a long-time scoutmaster, an active Jaycee member, a shooting advocate, and an accomplished wood carver. He is also a community resource as a volunteer and a township board member in Cass County.

He became a builder of heavy construction equipment and was the shop manager for Ray Go Manufacturing. Ray Go was eventually purchased by Caterpillar, Inc. (CAT).

This story is about one of Junior's first major mechanical creations. The vehicle he built in 1960 was a "goes anywhere" vehicle. He developed it out of his love for hunting and also out of his frustration with water problems in the Bigfork area.

Because of water holes and poor equipment, reaching his favorite hunting spot was a problem. With too many waterholes and too much gear to carry, it was an issue to be resolved.

Chapter 10
"Creation of a "Swamp Buggy"
Junior Sjodin

Over a period of eight years I had lived through the Bigfork mud, deep snow, and the equipment that would on too many occasions breakdown. Our deer hunting camp was located approximately one and a half miles east of the 'minimum maintenance' road. If there was excessive snow or rain it was a long walk transporting our supplies and gear.

While hunting ducks with my friend Bob, in the Federal Dam area I spotted a small track driven caterpillar style machine. It was manufactured in Canada by a company called 'Bombardier.' I took a good look at the way it was built. It had two tracks with the driver and the motor positioned between them.

The 'Ranger,' another similar style machine, manufactured on Minnesota's iron range only had room for one person. With it you could pull a trailer. Both machines certainly could work. Both were too limited in what they could do. I decided they had merit, but I could do better.

After seeing the Bombardier, the Ranger and several other different off the road vehicles, I knew I could build a "goes anywhere" vehicle. In fact I became convinced I could develop a better machine for our purposes and use at Bigfork. I decided the machine I built would have to have room to seat two or three people and would have a box that you could load with the food and other gear needed at our camp.

At Northern Pump where I worked I started talking it up with my duck hunting friend Bob. As we talked I was getting more and more ideas. The more we talked the more I was starting to know what would be needed to make a track vehicle. As I shared ideas with my friends and relatives they started coming forward with ideas and parts I could use in building the machine.

My friend Bob even offered me a 1935 Ford car. It had a 60 hp. V-8 engine; it would be perfect for powering such a machine. With my growing collection of ideas and a power train for such a machine I now needed to design the machine.

The more I got into the planning stage it became apparent that this was not an overnight project. It might take years to assemble the final product. I started to evaluate the resources I had available.

I was a trained welder with several years of layout experience. If I were to succeed both skills would be needed. The friends I worked with also had skills in the layout, fabrication and welding of steel products.

They would be a resource to help me with any design or manufacturing problems I might have. My neighbor Doug, who also hunted with us, volunteered his garage for the project. Doug also had good mechanical skills. Later on Doug actually became my right hand man for the project.

I kept talking the project up with my friends and relatives. One of my relatives who lived on Minnesota's Iron Range said he had access to discarded heavy duty conveyor belts. He described them as being approximately 1/2 inch thick and 20 to 30 inches wide. He was sure finding 40 feet or more of the discarded belting would be no problem. I knew the way he described the belting it would be the perfect material for the tracks and sprockets I would need to build.

My dream of building a machine that "goes anywhere" was moving in a positive direction. There still were many unanswered questions. I was, however, lining up the resources I needed to bring my dream to fruition. It's hard to describe how everything was designed. Some of it was the actual designs I put on paper during the planning stage. The rest of it was either changes that were needed because of our knowledge of mechanics or else trial and error.

The engine, driveshaft and rear end were fairly basic. How high the engine needed to be mounted was tackled fairly early. We needed to keep it as high as possible. The creeks, swamps and waterholes we would drive through or cross required us to make sure we had adequate clearance. Keeping the distributer and condenser dry is critical for the 1935 Ford V-8 engine.

A track vehicle requires a dual braking system. Two separate break cylinders, lines, levers and brake drums are needed so that the machine can be turned. Without such a system the driver of a track vehicle cannot turn the machine. Forward and backward are not the only required directions.

One of the major problems was designing, spacing and constructing the two tracks. The tracks had to be properly designed and laid out so that the cross cleats fit into the notches of the sprockets properly. If not, excessive wear and/or binding of the tracks or sprockets would be the result.

The cross cleats and the sprockets had to line up perfectly. When we were finally able to have the tracks working properly with the sprockets we knew we were making good progress. We also knew we would have less wear and tear on the cleats and sprockets.

To build the tracks I used the discarded conveyor belting that my relative picked up at the iron mines. The cross cleats I needed for tracks were more difficult. They required heavy metal, steel that was bent, and then formed to their proper shape.

Where I worked they had the machinery to cut, form and bend the steel. I was able to have the 60 cross cleats made using their equipment.

Forming the cleats was a job my friend Bob took over. The actual design for the cleats was done by Bob and me. We made a die to use for the proper bending of the steel. Each cleat required a piece of steel 3/16"x3 ½"x18"es. Scrounging up 60 pieces of scrap steel required some time. Once we assembled the 60 pieces of steel required for the cleats Bob took over the bending and forming needed to make the cleats usable.

At this point I had the sixty cleats and the four strips of belting I needed. We now had to make the needed one hundred twenty inside retainers. They also required bending and the proper forming so that they would keep the tracks in place and properly guided on their three idlers.

The steel needed for these we found in the scrap pile at the 'LaHasse' company. Doug and I both worked part time for that company. The company was building bodies for dump trucks. Any scrap metal behind the cutoff shears, the company told us was ours for the taking.

Finding the one hundred twenty pieces of 1/8"x2"x8" steel only took one Saturday morning. At the dump truck body shop behind the cutoff shears we found all the steel we needed. The bending and forming of the inside retainers was done in Doug's garage. We were able to do this bending and forming because Doug had a coal-fired forge and welding equipment in his garage.

To assemble the two tracks required the following materials.

Four six-inch by 24 feet of heavy belting

60 cross cleats and 120 idler retainers'

Approximately, 240 bolts, washers and nuts.

The sprockets were made out of a piece of 1/4 inch steel plate and had the heavy conveyor belting bolted to their sides. The belting was at least 1/4 inch wider than the steel plate. As I said earlier the belting cut down on wear and tear, it also cut down on the clatter and noise associated with tracked vehicles.

The amount of drilling the steel and the belting was a time consuming job. The lining up of the holes, pushing the bolts through the belting, retainers, the cross cleats and then securing them with the washers and nuts was no less time consuming.

The part time work Doug and I were doing at the LaHasse Company was really paying off. We had access to scrap steel and the machines needed to form it. With the scrap steel and the machines we were able to form the parts we needed for the Swamp Buggy's frame.

The various parts for the frame were assembled in Doug's garage. We then were able to set the 1935 Ford 60 hip engine in place on the frame. Once the engine was in place I recruited my Dad's help. Dad knew what to do to properly mount and tune the engine. It took a little puttering around, but dad was able to get it running smoothly.

Once we had the engine running we knew immediately it needed mufflers. Two were installed, one for the exhaust on each of the two manifolds. The idlers were automobile wheels and tires bolted to the sides of the machines frame. They worked very well and rode well on the "buggies" tracks and cleats.

The front to rear picture shows the track, idlers, cleats and motor arrangement. The set of idlers on the back is a complete unit that can be moved forward and back. This feature allowed us to remove and/or tighten the tracks. Also when we needed to transport the Buggy we needed the flexibility that this feature offered us. It was a great system and served us well.

The whole system of the tracks and idlers worked well. We even came up with a bonus. By removing the tracks, the rear idlers and then adding a tow bar the whole machine became its own trailer. The tracks were hinged at one point and by pulling the pins they could be laid flat, rolled up and put in the Buggy's box. It rolled on its idlers.

On one of our trips we did not secure the rear idlers properly and they fell off while we were in transit. When we discovered the idlers were gone we retraced our journey back on Highway 65. We were out of business until I could remake the assembly for the back two idlers.

I never did find out what happened to them. They were lost somewhere along highway 65 between Mora and Spring Lake Park. Maybe someone reading this story can give me a call and tell me where they found them.

Because our plan entailed mounting the engine in the rear of the swamp buggy the rear end ended up in the front. The differential was fitted backwards between the two. That way our sprockets were in the front of the swamp buggy. By doing this, the track was just ahead of the idlers, and the front was actually lifted a few inches off the ground.

Later on a second transmission was installed between the engine and rear end, (which now was the front end). By doing this we were able to gain power and also slow the machine down. We also raised the two rear idlers several inches to keep more track off the ground. These changes made turning easier. The changes also allowed us to turn without the machine rolling off its tracks.

When Doug and I completed the creation we called it the "Swamp Buggy." To me it was an attractive machine. I discovered early that you did not let just anybody drive the Swamp Buggy.

Why you ask? The breaking system and the cross cleats were equally good. If you over break the machine on one side or the other you could throw off a track. Fixing a track and realigning it always meant extra work.

The Swamp Buggy was truly a 'goes anywhere' machine. I used the machine for duck hunting, deer hunting, hauling materials, checking out logging roads near our camp and sightseeing. It was a machine that was functional, fun and offered me a great learning experience.

After we completed the machine I left it with Bob at Federal Dam, Minnesota. Bob used it in the fall when hunting and trapping. One of the highlights I enjoyed was when Bob and I drove a mile across the Leach Lake bog.

We were able to drag the canoe we would use and fill it with our dogs, guns and other equipment. We also had three poles with us. They were 3 to 4 inches in diameter and at least 20 feet long. We placed the three poles on the ground in front of the Swamp Buggy, drove up on them and actually parked on the three poles.

Without the poles to set on, the Swamp Buggy would have settled into the bog 20 to 24 inches. By setting on the poles we only settled 5 or 6 inches into the bog. If we allowed the Swamp Buggy to settle in 20 inches or more we would be getting too close to the distributor and condensers.

Our trips across the Leach Lake bog also gave us a chance to make any needed changes. After these trips I decided to slow the machine down by installing the second transmission. By slowing the machine down it was easier to control and more power was accomplished.

One of the first real tests at Bigfork was when Doug and I spent all day hauling building materials from the minimum maintenance road to our camp. Doug and I were doing the loading, hauling and unloading of the materials for a hunting shack.

We were not, however, as fast as Punky and Bob were at nailing the materials together for the hunting shack that was being built. They always thought it was funny when we'd get back and they asked, "Where have you been all this time?"

Because I let Punky and Bob use the machine from time to time they were always causing me to make repairs on the Swamp Buggy. One time I got a call that they had taken a nose dive with the Swamp Buggy into a spring area on the road heading north to what we call the log cabin area.

At the time I had to call my duck hunting friend, Bob who was in Federal Dam to help me. He had recently purchased a Ranger that was manufactured in Pengilly, Minnesota. With the Ranger we were able to pull the Swamp Buggy out of the spring hole. So much for the GOES ANYWHERE machine; we found out it could get stuck.

The next Bigfork experience was in the same swamp, the one leading up to the log cabin area, where I had to pull it out of the spring hole. I was driving and heard a loud knock in the engine. We had burned out a rod bearing. I left the Swamp Buggy where it was sitting. As luck would have it we had made it to the high ground in the center of the Swamp. It was an area where my middle son, Paul had recently shot his first deer. The Swamp Buggy was left out there for several months.

During the winter once everything froze up we were able to go back and retrieve the engine. We used our snowmobiles and our friend Stanley used his big sled to help pull it out. After rescuing the engine I took it to Minneapolis and had it rebuilt. To have the engine overhauled was a problem. Parts for a 1935 Ford V8 were hard to find. By the time I completed the overhaul I had another $600 invested in the engine.

A month later I returned with the repaired engine and reassembled the Swamp Buggy. The engine never ran better than it did after the overhaul.

After having the Swamp Buggy for about ten years I parked it in my Mable Lake garage. That winter the head gaskets leaked. The antifreeze worked its way into the pistons and other parts of the motor. The engine seized up and was never used again.

When I moved from Mable Lake to my current home on Portage Lake I hauled the Swamp Buggy and placed it behind our syrup shed. It has rested there for over 30 years.

The Swamp Buggy will always be remembered as the machine that would go anywhere; well, 'almost anywhere.' It definitely has a warm spot in my heart.

I know building the machine that we named the "Swamp Buggy" had a significant part in my personal and professional development. It also was a project in which my family was involved. They also enjoyed the benefits it offered and the travels we took with it.

Pictured, when the Swamp Buggy was first built, are Junior and Doug. A future hunter, Son, Mike, was trying it out too.

Note: In November of 2013, I gave two of my nephews the discarded Swamp Buggy. Their plan is to restore it.

Chapter 11

UNSOLICITED PUBLICITY

The <u>Western Itasca Review</u> Newspaper
and Charlie Turnbull

Once in a while, something totally unexpected happens, as it did to us in 1961. Six of us were packed and had driven into Bigfork to get a bite to eat and gas up before heading home. We had our Swamp Buggy in tow, our six deer loaded and we were ready to head for home. As we were walking up to our cars, a lady stopped us and started asking questions about our hunting.

We asked her who she was. It turned out she was in Bigfork looking for local news as a reporter for the <u>Western Itasca Review</u>. The paper is located in Deer River. "What do you want to know", was our response. She asked us where we were from, where we hunted, about our obvious success; she took some pictures and asked several other questions.

We gave her the information and thought little of it until she sent us the next week's paper. There on the front page was a picture of us standing by our Swamp Buggy and the six deer we were successful in harvesting that season.

The reporter mailed the November 16, 1961 edition of the <u>Western Itasca Review</u> to Junior. He shared it with all who were involved in the 1961 hunt. All of us were pleased with the recognition we received because of the article and the picture that accompanied it. We thought the part of the caption, "-the hunters from Minneapolis know how to hunt deer..." was a nice touch.

The 1961 hunt was the second year in a five-year period where our hunting exceeded our expectations. You always hope to fill the tags you have been issued; it just doesn't happen that way every year.

It was only a few years later, because of several harsh winters and a dwindling deer herd, that the State of Minnesota tried several types of seasons. The most common one was what we all know as a "bucks only" season.

Another type of season the DNR tried was letting the hunters choose a set of days during the month of November. Depending on the dates the hunters chose to hunt, they would have three to five days of hunting time.

One year they even closed it totally. Not a smart move that year when the DNR lost 450 thousand license sales.

The current system that the Department of Natural Resources uses is a combination of "bucks only" coupled with a "lottery drawing" for antlerless permits in the various areas/zones throughout the State. By using this system, they have been able to maintain 'known' starting dates for hunting and at the same time maintain a fairly stable deer herd.

No matter what system the DNR used or uses the Lean-To-Boys have adjusted, and usually have had some very good deer hunting. The five-year period from 1960 through 1964 was the most consistent and best five years of hunting we have had.

Pictured, l to r, are Merlyn, Junior, Clarence and Punky Sjodin, Doug Mitchell and Charlie Turnbull.

The photo and caption the *Western Itasca Review* printed

in 1961 were a good depiction of the hunts we had over that period of time.

If we never formally said thank you to the <u>Western Itasca Review</u> staff and paper for that article, we are doing so at this time

Charlie's note: Thank You, <u>The Western Itasca Review,</u> for a VERY MEANINGFUL picture and story!

Chapter 12

THE EARLY 1960S

Charlie Turnbull

From 1960 through 1964, the Lean-To-Boys experienced some of the finest deer hunting in Minnesota. It was the period of time, when filling our tags was a routine event. During that five-year period of time, we not only filled our tags, we filled one to three tags, for the Smith hunting party.

Minnesota allows party hunting and we took advantage of the opportunity it offered. In that way, as devoted deer hunters, we could spend more time in the field deer hunting.

It was also the time in our lives when we were able to plant our feet more firmly on the ground. We had a better sense of direction in all aspects of our life.

Junior was hired by Ray Go Manufacturing as it's first employee. He had the opportunity to build the company's first road compaction machine, called the Ray Go "Rascal." As the Ray Go plant manager, he was in the process of helping that firm become a successful competitor in the heavy-equipment business.

Punky, who is Junior's brother, joined the Marines in the spring of 1958 and was discharged in 1961. He was again hunting with us on a regular basis.

In 1962, I completed my formal schooling at the University of Minnesota. After six years, it was a great relief to have college behind me. In 1963, Junior and I both completed our family's expansion.

Clarence was actively hunting with us through 1962. After 1962, he gave it up and told us he had taught us well and we were on our own. The basic nucleus for our hunting camp between 1959 and 1970 was Junior, Punky, Doug and I. There were several others who hunted with us for a few years and then dropped out.

During that period of time, the percentage of whitetail bucks we harvested was very high. It was almost unbelievable how high that percentage was.

It was Punky, however, who set our camp record of five bucks in one season. His record, set over 50 years ago, in 1962, has not been broken. As you view the following photos, you will notice the predominance of antlered whitetails.

In the photo, it shows Punky tagging one of his five bucks.

The photos tell the story of some great hunts. They also depict a period of time when taking photos of our harvested animals was more acceptable than it is now.

It must be noted that, prior to 1961, taking photos of our successes was not a high priority. Doug, after he joined us in 1959, was the one who was good with the camera. He took most of our photos throughout the 1960s.

1961 was the second of five outstanding years of deer hunting. Once we had our six bucks in 1961 and our six licenses filled, we contacted members of the Smith party to see if they had their licenses filled. They didn't and they welcomed our help in filling several of their licenses.

We were happy with the extra deer hunting we were offered by joining in with the Smith party. After all, it allowed us to have more deer hunting time. During that period of time most of us were harvesting more than our share of the antlered animals.

As I indicated before, Minnesota allows party hunting. Party hunting doesn't appear to affect the size of the deer herd. Each year, Minnesota has approximately 500,000 deer hunters. The success ratio usually runs in the 35 to 50% range (see Ch. 32).

With the 1961 hunt behind us, our deer loaded, the "Swamp Buggy" in tow and our trailer loaded with gear, it was time to head home.

The following photos say it better than a thousand words, ever could. The photo, of 5 hanging buck deer, is one of the best we ever took. 1962 was another great year of buck hunting by the Lean-To-Boys. In the photo, the corner of the 8'x8' fish house can be seen. We used it in our camp during the early 1960s. The fish house, along with a tent, for several years, provided our sleeping and cooking areas.

1962 and 1963 were also very good to our hunters. They were seasons when we filled our tags in the first two or three days. By noon on the second day in 1962, we had five of our six licenses filled. We only had one left to fill. Over time, we discovered that if we filled 50 to 60 percent of our licenses the first day, we usually filled on Sunday or Monday. That five-year period from 1960 through 1964 proved the point.

Two hundred pound 'field-dressed' whitetails are few and far between. We harvest one every once in a while. The Bigfork area is one of the most productive in Minnesota for large whitetails.

In 1958, Charlie harvested a buck that weighted in at 204 pounds. In 1955, Junior harvested a buck, one that a knowledgeable person estimated too weigh be between 250-260 pounds.

The big buck, I shot in 1964, third from the left, officially weighed in at 234 pounds.

Our hunting party, over the years, has grown from six hunters to 12 to 14 hunters. It is my personal opinion that a party of six is the ideal size for a deer hunting camp.

As I indicated earlier, Junior and I completed the expansion of our families in 1963. This meant that, as our children became 12 years of age, our party would expand. That expansion started in 1965, when Junior's oldest boy, Chuck, became 12 years of age. It was more and more evident that we needed better accommodations. We also knew that over the next four to seven years we would have another five of our offspring joining us. It definitely was time to start considering some changes in the way we camped.

We needed to come up with a more permanent and usable shelter. One major problem was the fact that we did not own any land in our hunting area. We made a decision to take a chance and build a shelter on public land.

The area where we made our first camp in 1952 was still our favorite camping spot. The decision to build a cabin at that location was an easy one to make. The development and planning for the project was taken over by Punky, with the aid of his friend Bob.

The care and processing of our venison is a high-priority item for the Lean-To-Boys. It is our feeling if you're going to take the time to prepare and do the work required for a successful hunt, it doesn't make sense not to take proper care of the venison. It all starts with proper field dressing and cooling of the meat. The packaging of the meat after its cut up is also an important step. What we have found works well is to use cling wrap as the first layer around the meat. It basically seals the meat and cuts down on the freezer burn. The second layer is regular freezer paper. Utilizing this system, we've been able to keep meat frozen for up to a year.

Hanging your animals not only aids in cooling, it allows for some of the excess blood to drain out. Notice how our animals are thoroughly opened up so that the animal's body heat can be lowered rapidly.

We always process our own animals. By processing our own, we always knew the quality of our venison was first class. It was cut the way we liked it, and we knew what and whose meat went into the hamburger.

Note: There are a couple of things we avoid in the process of butchering the meat. The first thing we know is the fat of the animal carries most of the wild taste of venison. Because of that, we remove the fat from the meat. We also try to "de-bone" as much of the meat as we can. It is our feeling that freezing bone and fat are a waste of electrical energy.

Junior's garage always worked out best for us. In the garage, we could set up the tables and other equipment needed to do the butchering properly.

The most rewarding part of the process is enjoying a great venison meal. To prepare venison, the most important rule when frying or roasting the meat is 'not' to overcook it.

Here are several recipes that we like:
Recipe #1, Fried deer heart.
Cut the heart into strips (about ½" - 5/8")
Dredge them in flour or corn meal with salt and pepper added
Fry the strips in hot butter (250 degrees) until lightly browned. Remove from heat and serve.

Note: do not overcook the heart; it is best if served rare to medium. We do liver at our camp as an appetizer the same way we do the heart.

Recipe #2, Fried venison steak.

Cut your meat into 1" thick slices.

Frying steaks, after the cutting is done, is very similar to Recipe #1. Fry at 250 degrees, add salt, pepper and garlic salt.

Note: Again, do not overcook the steak, rare is better. Soda crackers and/or potato chips, crushed and thoroughly crumbled, work well for the outer coating of the venison.

Recipe # 3, Venison summer sausage. This is popular with most hunters. It usually requires somebody to mix the meat and/or smoke it to properly process it.

We wish each of you good hunting, proper preparation of the venison and great eating.

Chapter 13

MY OLD MAN

I first met Junior's father, Clarence, in 1950. He had just returned home from overseas. Clarence had been working on construction projects as a heavy machine-operator. On most of those projects, he had to sign up for a year or two. If you completed the contract, there usually was a bonus involved.

This was a period of time shortly after World War II. All during World War II, he had worked in Alaska. With the start of the war in the winter of 1941, there was a great need for mechanics and heavy equipment operators. For a ten-year period of time, Clarence worked in Alaska and on various overseas projects. After he returned home to Minnesota in 1950, he found work in the Twin Cities. His line of work always involved heavy equipment.

The door to the Sjodin house was always open. If they were eating, there was always a place at the table for those of us who would occasionally drop in. Because Junior and I had become friends and had done a lot of hunting together, it was easy to get to know Junior's dad. He, too, was a hunter and outdoors man.

Chapter 13
My Old Man
1909- 1966
Junior Sjodin

My Dad was "the old man" in our deer hunting camp. He was a man who lived on adventure. Hunting and fishing were always a part of his life and personal interests.

Dad grew up in the Onamia and Milacs Lake area of Minnesota. He spent many hours hunting, fishing and trapping around Onamia's Rice Lake. In the early 1900s boys grew up rather rapidly. My Dad was no exception.

At 17 he left home and took a job as a lumberjack in the area near Bigfork and Effie, Minnesota. To survive lumberjacks had to grow up fast. One of his early camp friends was a gentleman by the name of Charlie Larson.

Charlie was a camp cook but he also ran a hunting camp in the Effie area. Charlie got frustrated one day with his hunters late in the season. The hunters were not harvesting any deer.

Dad told me, Charlie grabbed his 35 Remington automatic and took into the woods. Charlie returned with five deer hearts all from bucks. From that day forward he was known as "Buck Larson".

Dad told me the feat was even more impressive because Buck had lost his hearing in an explosion. Evidently he was too close when the dynamite exploded. Dad explained back then a lot of dynamite was used to remove stumps.

Evidently while hunting he was able to make up for his hearing loss with his eyes and his awareness of the deer and their habits. Dad told me in 1952, if Buck was still alive and we could find him he would be our best resource for finding a place to hunt.

Saturday night after the men got paid most of them headed for Craigsville. Craigsville was the favorite 'watering hole' for the lumberjacks. Craigsville offered moonshine, showgirls, and was a great place to let off steam.

It was a little town about 2 miles north of Effie. Effie, another small town ten miles north of Bigfork, Minnesota, on Highway 38 was a couple miles closer but not as wide open as Craigsville.

For the lumberjacks Saturday night in Craigsville, Dad told me, was one riotous affair. Back then it offered lots of moonshine, women, and guns. The combination of moonshine, women and guns made Saturday nights at Craigsville a riotous affair. Craigsville in the 1920s was a place where shootings, accidents and random unsolved murders were routine events.

Dad told me of how the authorities would use chicken wire and stretch it across the Big Fork River to collect the bodies as they floated down stream. When this happened the authorities would enlist the moonshine runners and get them to take the bodies to the pier in Duluth and dump them in Lake Superior.

Dad never mentioned making any of these runs. Who knows what really happened in the early 1920s and 1930s.

Dad said there were women in Craigsville but not enough. More fights and shootings were caused by the lumberjacks fighting over the showgirls. The first night Dad went to Craigsville his eyes were opened wide as he watched scantily clothed women dancing and prancing on the stage.

For my Dad it was not only a new experience, it was a real eye-opener. Certainly not anything he had previously seen in his young life up to that point. Dad had a lot of experience hunting, fishing, and trapping before he became a lumberjack. He had little experience with women previous to his Craigsville visits.

Dad and his friend Leonard joined on as lumberjacks in the mid-1920s. Dad's bosses name was George. George had a four-door Packard automobile. It was a great automobile and it was the perfect auto for making the moonshine runs.

Like I said earlier Dad never mentioned that he made any of these runs from Craigsville to Duluth and back. Dad, however, always kept his eyes open and his ear to the ground. He knew what was going on with the activities in Craigsville.

Dad was aware of what was being done and said around the lumber camp. By doing so he knew what was going on around him. Knowing this about my dad, I always believed the stories he told me about Craigsville and his lumberjack days.

In 1952 Dad, Charlie and I made a trip to Bigfork, Minnesota. It was a September trip and we made a side jaunt to Craigsville. The building that housed the bar and show girls was still there. It was boarded up and showing the signs of years of neglect.

Craigsville was a town with a past. It had a very lively past at that. At least it was lively for those who survived the fights, brawls and shootings.

Dad told me his friend Leonard and he, their first winter, stayed at Buck Larson's cabin on Larson Lake. The two of them spent the winter trapping and fishing.

Dad particularly mentioned how hard it was to be able to spear fish during the winter. They had to chop the ice with an ax. If the ice was thick it took hours to get a hole big enough to use for spearing fish.

Back in those days Dad and Leonard didn't use a dark house, they used an old canvas. They would cover themselves and the hole to shut out the light. By doing that, they could watch their decoy and actually spear fish.

Any time they needed new gear, food or equipment they had to pull a sled several miles across country. Once in town they packed the sled with the gear and food they purchased and then headed back to their winter home on Larson Lake.

Dad married my mother during the Depression. I was born in 1933. In 1935 dad and my mother signed up on the government program aimed at establishing a colony in Alaska.

Each family was allowed one major appliance. My mother was the only one who thought a 'gas powered washing machine' would be better and more useful than a stove or any other appliance. My mother's gas driven washing machine was the most appreciated appliance in the new Alaskan colony.

This adventure required our family to build a house on the 40 acres we were homesteading. My dad thought this was working out fairly well. At least it went well until 7 December 1941 when the Japanese declared war on the United States.

My mother in 1942 packed up her brood and headed back to Minnesota. She didn't care for the Japanese planes flying overhead. Many Americans never realized that there was a war front and lots of fighting going on up and down the Allusion Islands and in Alaska.

Because of the war Dad was needed and stayed in Alaska. They needed heavy equipment operators to help build the Alaska Highway and other crucial projects for the war effort. During the 9 to 10 years Dad lived in Alaska, in addition to his work, he and his brother George did a lot of hunting.

One of my favorite stories was how they were able to shoot sheep 500 yards away. One of them would get in a good solid shooting position and take careful aim with their peep sight. The other, after the shot was taken, if it was a miss would watch with their binoculars to see where the bullet kicked up the dirt and dust. With this information it was fairly easy to zero in and hit the animal.

With this system they were successful hunters. Long shots were often necessary and this system worked very well for them. Because of my Dad's hunting experiences in both Minnesota and Alaska he was able to advise me on different ways to master cold weather.

By listening to his tales and hearing how he was able to stay warm, make fires and keep his clothing dry I found many grains of wisdom. His Ideas have helped me as I have ventured in the out-of-doors.

After W. W. II Dad followed the jobs that were opening up for heavy equipment operators and mechanics on the various islands in the Pacific Ocean. Dad worked overseas for approximately four or five more years. There was much cleanup work as well as new construction going on throughout the Pacific. America was expanding their domain in the world.

Dad returned home in 1950. He found work in the construction business in the Twin Cities. He almost always was working with heavy equipment.

When Dad realized that my buddies and I had hunted deer in southern Minnesota during the 1951 season he was a little upset. Dad told me, "Southern Minnesota is no place to hunt deer. It's too dangerous with all of those shotgun slugs bouncing around those hills and fields."

Go north was his advice. Dad's advice was sound and well taken. In 1952 my dad started planning with us a trip up north. Because of my Dad's experience in the Bigfork area that became our focal point in planning our first hunt in 1952.

Dad was one of the original four Lean-To-Boys. In 1953 and 1954 he took my younger brothers to our Bigfork camp for deer hunting. He truly was one of the Lean-To-Boys and "the old man" and mentor for all of us.

Chapter 14

ANOTHER BIG BUCK YEAR

Charlie Turnbull

1964, started out very much like the previous three years. It was a mild year with no snow. Not even a hint or chance of having snow the first weekend. It was the kind of year when sitting on your stand was a pleasant and warm experience. For Minnesota, it was another warm opening day in November.

I was doing just that, sitting on my stand that opening morning. I was enjoying the warmth of the morning sun. My stand was a very simple four foot by four foot platform. It was only off the ground about three and one-half feet. It was as basic as any stand you could have.

You could sit on it or stand on the platform. There were no rails to lean on or chairs to sit on. You had to stand on it or sit dangling your feet. I started out by sitting and enjoying the morning. Later, I stood for a spell, and when I got tired I would sit down again. Actually it was a very comfortable stand to sit on.

It was just about 10 a.m. when I heard a light snap of a twig. A deer was directly behind me. When I turned and moved, the buck saw me. He froze momentarily, then turned and leaped away. I took a quick shot, but missed. Having to twist and turn around threw me off balance and off target.

When a deer comes up to you from your back it usually has the advantage. This is especially true when you're using a low stand, such as the one I was sitting on that morning.

I'm sure that buck noticed me the moment I turned. If my stand had been eight feet in the air, he may not have seen me. It wasn't, so he did see me. I had to play the hand I was dealt. It was in a good place for a stand, but I messed up a good opportunity. I was just facing the wrong direction.

It's possible that the buck may have walked right past me had I not moved. If the deer would have walked past me, he would have been in the clearing that I was overlooking. That buck, a six pointer, was a nice animal; basically not a monster, just a nice buck.

On opening day, I hate to miss an opportunity like the one I was offered. It doesn't start your hunting on the right foot. It is nice to connect the first morning. When I missed that good opportunity my spirits took a downward tumble. When something like that happens, I always want to know what I could have done differently. I believe there was little I could have done differently once I heard the twig snap. The shot I took certainly could have been more accurate. I probably had more time than I thought; I only had to take the time. Once I saw the deer I probably could have stood up, turned and still have had time for a longer, but more accurate, shot.

One thing I knew from the buck's midmorning movement, the "rutting" season was in progress. When the bucks are moving mid-morning in the early part of November they are usually seeking does.

One thing I always have told the other hunters; 'If you get one good opportunity, the deer does not owe you anything." After all, I missed. The deer showed up, and my job was to take advantage of the situation. I had my chance. Hopefully, I'd get another.

An hour later, Junior walked over to my stand. He had heard my earlier shot and waited to come over and see what had happened. I reviewed my lost opportunity with him.

He told me nothing was happening over by his "well stand" and he got bored and wanted to find out what happened when I shot. He was talking about walking a few of the logging roads after he left my stand.

As we were chatting and discussing my earlier miss, we heard a deer breaking twigs and small sticks. The deer's hooves where loudly thumping the ground. He was rapidly heading our way. The noise was a distinct rumble. The deer was in a hurry to distance himself from something, and he was moving at a fast pace toward the two of us.

When we first heard the deer coming, he had to be 200 yards to the north. He was coming through an area of grass and woods just north of my stand. There was no doubt he was coming our way.

Most of the time bucks are sneaking and being very quiet. This one was not. Somebody north of us must have jumped him to have him move so rapidly. As he came closer the deer's thumping, as he was breaking the brush and sticks as he hit the ground, got louder and louder. This deer was not a small deer. I had never heard a deer crashing through the underbrush like this deer was doing. He was not sneaking up on me like the one did an hour earlier. This buck was making his presence known in advance.

Earlier, when Junior arrived, I got off my perch and stood up. We were both standing there when we heard the buck coming our way. We both moved to face the oncoming deer. At that time, both of us were ready to take a shot at the deer. The buck bounded into the small clearing and stopped in his tracks. For him, it was the wrong thing to do. Junior shot first. Then an unexpected thing happened. Junior missed the buck at 30 yards. I shot immediately after him. My shot was right on target. The buck hunched up and fell right where he had been standing.

It was hard to believe that Junior missed. He was using his trusty Winchester model 94, lever action 32 special. He usually never missed. It is hard to know what happens when you mess up a shot like that.

In a way, when two hunters are standing next to each other, it creates a slight bit of competition, especially when a buck, or any deer, shows up as that one did. I know I was a happy hunter to have been the one to harvest that particular buck. I had just messed up a shot an hour earlier, and if I had missed this opportunity, I would have really been down in the dumps.

In a way I almost did miss out, but God must've been looking out for me. If he was not looking out for me, he probably felt sorry for me. Who knows? I was just happy with the outcome. This buck was the second buck that I have harvested that weighed over 200 pounds. The first one was in 1958. He weighed in at 204 pounds. This one was significantly larger, weighing in at 234 pounds.

It was an official weight taken at a place where they were having a big buck contest. I thought I really had a chance to win the contest until I found out another buck had weighed in at 275 pounds.

The rack on this buck was a good one. The four evenly-developed and long tines on each side of the buck's antlers made it a good-looking rack. It was not a monster-sized rack. It was the evenness and heavy beams that made it special.

My plan was to mount the rack and hang it in my home. I never got around to it. Many years later, I lost the rack, and several others, when my barn burned down.

I keep thinking about those three racks I lost in that fire years ago. Just maybe in the near future I'll have the privilege of harvesting another big buck. In the meantime, I will live with several memories of big bucks, the ones that offered me a chance to harvest them.

Each year when I take the journey to my stand, I always hope another big buck will come into one of my shooting lanes. In the meantime, while I'm waiting for the next big one (or any deer), I'll take the time to enjoy the chickadees, brush wolves, ruff grouse, weasels, raccoons and mink that do show up occasionally.

It is always a pleasure being comfortable in my stand, even if the deer forget to show up. There is always another animal or two to enjoy watching as they work their way through the woods.

Chapter 15

LEAVING A PILE OF ENTRAILS

Punky invited his friend Bob to join our hunting party in 1966. At Anoka High School, they both were active on the wrestling team. Everybody who knew Bob back then thought he would become a state champion wrestler, and he probably would have had he remained in school. In the eleventh grade they both dropped out of school.

Shortly after dropping out of school, Bob enlisted in the Navy. In the Navy he became an airplane mechanic and wrestled on the team representing his base.

For over forty years, he had been known by his friends as "Bone Crusher" Bob. Junior and others thought it was because of Bob's reputation for fighting. He did have the reputation as a "bar room brawler."

When the Lean-To-Boys gathered together on October 17, 2009 for a reunion, Bob clarified how he earned the "Bone Crusher" moniker. All of us thought he had been in a fight and had broken some guy's arm, and that is not how he earned that moniker. Bob clarified for me and the others how he really earned that moniker.

Evidently, at one of his high school wrestling matches, his opponent's arm was accidently broken. Even at the high school level, accidents like that happen. The "Bone Crusher" tag was then given to Bob. For many years most people were operating under the wrong assumption for the term "Bone Crusher."

Later on, he started working for Junior at Ray Go Manufacturing Company. Ray Go manufactured heavy road equipment for highway and other earth-moving projects. The company was bought and sold several times. It finally ended up as a part of CAT.

Because of Bob's work skills and dedication to the company, the company had a good employee, and he did well working for them. It was a period of time when he was settling down.

Bob harvested his first buck when he was sitting on Punky's fender stand. The fender had been from a discarded Model "T" car. It had been left behind by the early loggers in the area. Punky salvaged the fender from the model T's remains and he used it as a backless chair. When not in use, he moved it to the side of the logging road.

The stand is known as the "fender stand." Its location is on a logging road that goes north and south and has an east/west survey line crossing it. By sitting there, you can see in all four directions; i.e., four shooting lanes. Over the years, it has proven to be one of our more productive stands.

Chapter 15
Leaving a Pile of Entrails
Bob Sodman

My buddy Punky invited me to hunt with him, Clarence, Junior, Charlie and Doug. The hunting party consisted of five experienced hunters and me. Punky told me about some of the great deer hunting the Lean-To-Boys had during the 1950s and 1960s. It was the best offer to go hunting that I had ever received, so I gave it a try.

I hunted with them for 10 years. My first hunt with the Lean-To-Boys was in 1966. The camp located several miles east of Bigfork was in a very nicely wooded area. To be truthful the area was very nice. At least I thought it was a rather nice area. Beyond that there was not much to talk or brag about.

At the campsite there was a flimsy looking fish house. The fish house along with a tent had been used as cook kitchen and sleeping quarters for the hunters for a half a dozen years.

Several weeks before the deer season we made several work party trips to Bigfork. The purpose of the trips was to build a small cabin. The cabin was to be erected in such a way that you could go directly from the cabin into the fish house. In that way we would have good access to the gear we stored in the fish house.

The cabin we built was only twelve by sixteen feet. On the east wall we built in six bunks. They were six feet long, thirty inches wide, about two feet high and stacked three bunks high, one on top of each other. They reminded me of my Navy days.

The windows for the cabin were only sixteen inches tall but they extended most of the way across the top part of the north wall. In the early morning and evening hours the light coming in was minimal. We had to use propane lighting and/or Coleman lanterns all the time inside the shack.

The center part was reserved for our table and chairs. Realtors talk about their 'great rooms' in the houses they are trying to sell to other people. They had nothing on our new shack. We truly had a great room. Who else had a room with their beds, heating plant, kitchen, dining room and living room all in one room? We truly had a "great room" with only one drawback, no indoor plumbing.

To build this "great room" took more than just a few weekends of work. Punky who is a carpenter had been scrounging building materials from every job site he worked on. Any time a board or piece of lumber was discarded Punky took it home.

On big jobsites there are lots of pieces of building material that can be used. Many times they are discarded because to use them costs more than they are worth. When that happens they are discarded. Building this little cabin was not going to cost a lot of money. It would just take extra effort to work with the discarded building materials.

The first weekend we actually planned to go to Bigfork had arrived. We loaded our trailers with the available building materials, windows and the tools we would need. Four of us, Junior, Doug, Punky and I took off for Bigfork.

When we got there Punky and I nailed, sawed, measured, and once in a while had to re-measure a board. Eventually we had the frame work of a cabin. Junior and Doug did the hauling of the materials.

Punky and I were so fast that by the time Junior and Doug returned they would find us sitting down having a cool beer. We always had to ask them when they returned, "Why did it take you so long to get back?"

After all the beer we drank, it was amazing that we were doing a pretty good job of constructing the small cabin. Back in those days we were known to have a brew or two. Since that time I lost my taste for one. It probably was for the best.

When we finished using all the material we had with us that first weekend, we stood back and admired our handy work. It wasn't a shrine but to us it sure looked good.

For many years the cabin and fish house provided the hunters with a place of shelter and a place for extra storage.

Several years later a twelve by sixteen foot addition was added to the cabin. The expansion doubled the size to sixteen by twenty four feet. The cabin now was twice as big as before. Over several years we went from six bunks to twelve. We even built in several shelves for our gear.

"Those Were the Years My Friend" were words in a Frank Sinatra song. Those same words summed up my feelings for the cabin and my 10 years at Bigfork.

That first year for me is the one I remember the best of the ten years I hunted with the Lean-To-Boys. I even have a hunting story or two to tell. My first story isn't about deer hunting. This first story is about my shooting a ruff grouse and the memorable events it triggered for me.

You know ruff grouse are exceedingly good to eat. I was walking a logging road with Junior. Pretty soon I spotted a grouse up in a poplar tree. Junior said, "Shoot it" which I promptly did.

After I retrieved the grouse, Junior suggested that I clean it before we go to the cabin. Another good idea, we did not need the feathers and the rest of the mess in camp.

I took out my Rambo style knife. This knife wasn't just any old knife. It was a heavy-duty set of tools. In addition to a big knife blade it had a scissors, screwdriver, bottle opener, pliers and it even had a plastic tooth pick. All of those tools were wrapped up in one magnificent tool I call a knife.

This was a man's knife. On a knife like this you knew the blade would be sharp. The blade could cut through anything that it touched.

I held the grouse by his head. I had his feathers off and entrails out by that time. With me holding his head and with his body hanging down I had my chance to sever the grouse's head from its body. With a mighty swing of the Rambo knife, I "cut my thumb off.'

Not my whole thumb, just the first 3/16 of an inch. Blood was everywhere. Most of the blood was mine. I never knew if I was successful in detaching the grouses head from its body.

Junior saw what happened and immediately took over. What he did with the grouse I do not know. I do know we had grouse as an appetizer for supper that night. He must have finished cleaning the grouse.

At our camp we only had a few Band-Aids for our first aid kit. We had no antiseptic in the cabin. Junior solved the problem. Junior found a very expensive antiseptic. He poured at least 2 ounces from my bottle of "Royal Crown Brandy" onto the end of my thumb.

It hurt so much I thought he wanted to kill me, or maybe I wanted him to kill me. The cut and blood was one, almost bearable hurt. The brandy antiseptic made it an unbearable hurt.

Somehow I lived with the cut and pain and headed for bed. Thankfully the bleeding had stopped and the Band Aid stayed in place. If I could go to sleep that would help. As soon as I lay down in my bunk, I knew I was in trouble. The throbbing started and it seemed to be worse.

Every time my heart would beat I could feel the pain on the end of my thumb. How that was possible with no end on my thumb I cannot tell you. I was hurting and I was not looking forward to the next day.

The plan was to have me walk out with Junior and use the fender stand. The fender stand I was told to sit on was one of the best. I wasn't sure with my sore thumb that using it or any stand was a good idea.

Juniors stand was less than a half mile from the fender stand. He walked me to the fender and made sure I was OK. He said have a seat and left. To my surprise the seat really was a fender.

It had been part of the remains of the car that was sitting on the side of the logging road. The car had been discarded about forty years earlier. It was rusty and lacked paint. The fender was still solid. It did not bend under my 180 pounds.

I sat there for 20 minutes or so wondering if my thumb would ever quit throbbing. A few moments later I was distracted by rifle shots. They were to the west of me. It was probably someone in the Smith party. They hunt the open fields and woods on Smith's farm. The reputation they had for shooting was poor. They usually had more misses then hits.

Being distracted only lasted a few minutes. Again my thumb had my attention. It was still throbbing. Another 20 to 30 more minutes went by. A movement in the brush to my west caught my attention.

The movement was a deer, a buck moving towards me. It was coming from the direction of the shots I heard earlier that morning. When the buck moved behind some trees I repositioned myself so that I could get a better shot. With the buck moving my way I forgot about my throbbing thumb.

Soon he was close enough to me to take a shot. He had been moving slowly and it appeared that he was being very cautious. I shot and he fell. Punky was right; the fender was a good stand.

Now I did have a problem. My Rambo style knife and I were not on good terms with each other; I was hurting. With a throbbing finger I was not in a good position to field dress my buck.

No problem, Junior was close by. I walked over to his stand and told him I had a nice buck. He had offered to help me; I took him up on his offer.

Junior used his own knife; he didn't want anything to do with my Rambo "thumb slashing" knife. With his own knife he did the job of field dressing the buck.

My job in helping him was to hold the bucks' legs so they were out of Junior's way as he field dressed the deer. In that way I was of some help to him.

As we were field dressing the buck Junior noticed a minor flesh wound on one of the buck's front feet. When we finished field dressing the deer we backtrack the deer about 100 yards. We started from the place where I first saw the buck.

Sure enough there was a blood trail but not enough to be serious to the deer. Junior pointed out that there was just enough blood for somebody to track the deer. Several hours had already gone by since I heard the early morning shooting. Apparently nobody was trailing the buck.

We headed back to camp dragging the buck. Where we field dressed the buck we left a big "pile of entrails".

I am pictured here with my whitetail buck.

Two hours later, close to noon, two members of the Smith party showed up in our camp. They claimed we had their deer. I did not know who they were. I asked them where they came from. At that point Junior stepped in and took over.

Junior told them, no way. They claimed they had followed the blood trail all morning and came to a gut pile. We acknowledged that I had shot the deer and there was a "pile of entrails." We explained to them that the deer was killed by me. We also explained and took the time to show them where the deer was hit by their hunter.

When they saw the minor injury on the deer's front foot they knew they had no claim to my buck. When a deer is hit and the wound is life-threatening there is usually more blood than a few droplets in his tracks. If the first wound had been serious we would have given up the deer.

They left knowing their so called "claim to fame" was groundless. I was the one who made the shot that put the deer down and put venison on my platter. The buck was good eating.

I still wonder what they thought the first two or three minutes when the trail they were following turned out to be a "Pile of Entrails." Someday I will ask. Till then I'll just smile as I think about it.

Chapter 16

PRE-HUNT MEETINGS

Chuck was the first of the third generation of hunters to join our camp. Grandpa Clarence represented the first, and Junior and I represent the second generation. Now, many years later, we are in the fourth generation of hunters. My, how time flies by.

Chuck takes his hunting seriously. He takes the time to do the needed prep work for each hunt. He also likes to keep track of what has happened from year to year. He took over from his dad the camp's log book. Since Doug dropped out, Chuck takes most of the photos every year.

He has a couple of stands that are his favorites. It is easy to have a favorite when they produce, and his do. The key is doing the prep work and keeping the stand in good repair, which he does.

Chapter 16
Pre-Hunt Meetings
Chuck Sjodin

I had my first opportunity to go hunting with my dad and his friends in 1965. In my mind it was a great under taking. One I had been looking forward to for several years. That first year we used an old fish house and tent for our shelter. The next year my uncle Punky and his friend Bob built a small cabin.

With the cabin available we did not need the tent, but we did continue to use the fish house. Sometimes the fish house had to be used for sleeping, but after the cabin was built that did not happen very often.

For several years, prior to my being twelve, I was able to sit in on the next years deer hunts preplanning meetings. My dad, Junior, would have the preplanning meetings at our house. That worked out real well for me because I could sit in and listen to what they were going to do.

Charlie, Doug, Punky and Dad were always there. Once in a while one or two other hunters would come to the meetings. It was evident to me they had been invited to go on that years hunting trip.

Nothing about the pre-hunt meetings was ever run the same from year to year. There was some similarity in the way the meetings progressed. Over time the meetings were following a similar pattern, kind of like the following scenario.

Food; everybody will bring a hot dish. Make sure it fits in a half gallon milk carton and that it is frozen. We will have heart for hors d'oeuvres, if we get a deer or two. We will also have munchies and grouse, if we get one.

Breakfast, the first day we're going to have our regular standby S.O.S. We have to make sure we have the Carnation Evaporated Milk; it's better than regular milk for our S.O.S. On the other days we are going to have pancakes, eggs, bacon and toast. We have to make sure we have peanut butter and jelly for the toast and for sandwiches.

Lunches will be each hunter's responsibility as far as what they want besides sandwiches. We will buy several kinds of luncheon meat, cheese, onions and condiments for the sandwiches. If you want candy bars, cookies or any other "Podunk" it's up to you to bring it.

Dinners each evening will require at least two of the hot dishes, we bring. If we need the hot dishes for lunch time meals, that will be okay too. The hot dishes will be served with bread-and-butter, canned fruit and vegetables. We should be in good shape for evening meals.

Dad went on and reviewed last year's food list. A few changes were made, we had to add figs. Figs, I never knew why for sure, somebody said it's a tradition. Something about Dad and Charlie and the Marine Corps deserts. Evidently they liked them.

After my dad reviewed the food list with everybody he made the needed additions and subtractions of the various foods. We moved on to other areas of discussion and planning for the hunt.

As a special note; by having our hot dishes packed in milk cartons and frozen they acted as a block of ice in our coolers. Whatever hot dishes were selected for the evening meal would be taken out of the coolers and allowed to thaw out. In hot weather that morning, if it was cold the night before.

<u>Deer camp gear</u>; the first question was, who is going to drive? Doug will drive, that way he can haul the swamp buggy. With six of us going, we need more than one car, who will it be? Punky can drive. He has a new pickup truck with four wheel drive. He can carry some of the gear in the truck bed.

Make sure the one hundred pound propane tank is in the back and tied down. The one at Camp is low and we need to make sure we have enough. We will fill it in Bigfork at Unger's repair shop on the way to camp.

New guys you are responsible for your own sleeping bags, blankets, rifles, shells, and whatever else you need for hunting. Remember at night it gets cold in the cabin.

Charlie sleeps on one of the low bunks with a stocking cap on his head. In that way he stays warm. It's better to have an extra blanket or two than to be cold and miserable.

Junior and Doug will work on the Swamp Buggy and make sure it's ready to go. Without the Swamp Buggy we would have to carry our gear. That is one thing we want to avoid doing.

"Anybody have any questions or comments? None, that's good. Meeting adjourned, let's have a beer".

That's the way our pre-hunt meetings would go. They usually covered the basic items; a lot of the details would be worked out between the hunters with phone calls and assignments made as they were needed.

Nothing was very formal, just some good hunters knowing what they were doing from their military and work training coupled with their experience hunting in the Bigfork area. The pre-hunt meetings were always interesting to me and I learned a lot listening to the stories that came up before, during and after the meetings.

<u>Memories</u>, #1. Another memory I have of that time period, has to do with our family dog. Her name was Babe, she was a yellow lab. Babe loved to hunt. When the shotguns came out she was right there with her tail wagging waiting for you to load her in the car. When it came to pheasants and ducks no other dog beat Babe.

Every fall, just before the start of the deer season, Dad would bring out his rifles and prepare to leave. Babe could never understand why he had these guns for deer hunting out and ready to go and left her at home. Dad would leave, Babe would sulk and whine and carry-on for an hour or two.

She knew somebody was going hunting and she was being left behind. I always felt sorry for her because I was having some of the same feelings myself. In my mind it was a real shame she and I had to stay home.

A deer hunting camp is not a good place to have a dog. One year Charlie brought his yellow lab to deer camp. Charlie had a rope to tie Barley up so he could leave and go to his stand opening morning. Barley whined and barked and was a real pain in the rear that morning.

The only way Charlie and the rest of us could keep him quiet was to keep the dog inside the cabin. It worked, but having a dog in camp is not what we needed. Once was enough, Barley stayed home after that trip.

#2. As I look back sometimes I wonder if kids get pushed too soon into big game hunting. Maybe it would be better if they had a chance to do more bird hunting prior to going deer hunting. On the other hand bird hunting in Minnesota is becoming a dying sport.

Pheasants and ducks are not as viable as they were fifty years ago. Ruff grouse are still available but there is more hunting pressure. Turkey hunting is very much on the rise, but it is more like deer hunting than walking in a woods or field for grouse or pheasants.

Deer hunting is the one area in which the opportunities are equally good today, maybe even better than they were fifty or sixty years ago. When the Lean-To-Boys first went deer hunting in the Bigfork area it was a prime area. Now there is good deer hunting throughout all of Minnesota.

In fact there are many areas of the state where hunters may take two or more deer at this time. This is one area where the DNR has done a good job. We all know habitat is crucial for any species if they are to thrive. In Minnesota deer have adjusted and adapted well throughout the state.

#3. If we are ever going to see a chance for better pheasant and duck hunting I have two suggestions. First encourage sportsmen to go out and purchase the questionable areas that farmers have for cropping, buy a "potential" pot hole. By doing this they could restore some of the potholes that are needed for pheasants, ducks and other wild life. Second allow landowners to be able to raise pheasants on their own land for their own hunting pleasure.

This would be easy to do. If a landowner raised two to three hundred pheasants and released them on their own land for their own private hunting, we know many of those birds would drift over to adjoining properties. In this way the pheasant count would increase, which in turn would help everybody.

By combining the two ideas, I think, in time we would be helping in rebuilding the sport of bird hunting. Just a thought, but maybe if you think about it and buy a potential pot hole, it just might work.

In the meantime, we can all enjoy deer hunting and the great outdoors. We can enjoy the camp talk and friendships we develop through hunting. Personally I'm looking forward to my next hunt.

Chapter 17

PAUL'S EXCITEMENT

Paul is Junior's third son. He was born in 1957, and would be eligible to hunt deer in 1969. His older brothers, Chuck and Mike, started hunting in 1965 and 1967 respectively; Paul had been hearing Lean-To-Boys deer hunting stories from early childhood. He now, as the younger brother, was hearing them from his older brothers.

In addition to the stories about deer hunting that Paul had been hearing from his dad and two brothers, he had participated in the skinning and butchering of the deer they brought home. Paul's father, Junior, would have all the harvested deer dropped off and hung up in the family garage. Usually on Tuesday or Wednesday evenings the Lean-To-Boy's would all gather to do the skinning and butchering of their deer.

It was during those times that Paul had the opportunity to help with the work. During those times, he also would hear the "embellished" hunting stories. Some of the stories were of big bucks, about a hunter getting lost, or of a missed shot. All the stories were good stories and sounded like the kind of fun Paul wanted to be a part of.

All the stories were ones Paul identified with, stories that added to his dreams about hunting with the Lean-To-Boys. In addition to being twelve years old, Paul knew that, to hunt deer, he had to pass a gun-safety course that is required by the State. For Paul, it was no problem. He took his gun-safety class and passed with flying colors. With the requirements of age and gun-safety behind him, he was now ready to go.

1969 was Paul's year to start hunting. His dreams would start to come true. Paul was ready to take his place as the newest Lean-To-Boy. Paul was excited, and his anticipation was overwhelming. Paul's story depicts the same anticipation and emotions youngsters go through when they are finally ready to become a first-time deer hunter. Paul's story is best when told by Paul. He lived it. He has told his story many times at camp and at family gatherings. He now shares it with you.

Chapter 17
Paul's Excitement
Or
"When Dreams, Excitement and Anticipation Meet Reality"
Paul Sjodin

Before I was twelve tears old I had heard many times that deer hunting was fun. Deer hunting was exciting and that it is the greatest hunting available in Minnesota. I had heard this many times from my Dad and his friends who hunted in Bigfork with the Lean-To-Boys hunting party. Now I was even starting to hear it from my older brothers.

I had helped butcher deer. Our family garage had become the center for butchering the deer taken on the hunts in northern Minnesota. I was given a dull knife, some meat scraps and ribs to cut on and clean up. My job was to scrape the meat from the ribs and venison scraps. What I salvaged would go into the hamburger.

Dad was particular in the knives he used, they had to be sharp. Why, I ask you, did I and my younger brothers get stuck using dull knives? Good question. I think it was to slow us down and keep us out of the way. The real hunters had come to work on the big pieces of venison. My brothers and I, at that time, saw it as a good start.

By being allowed to help with the butchering I did start to dream about deer hunting. Each year I was getting more excited about my going deer hunting. I took my gun safety class when I became twelve years old. The class psyched me up even more. I could see this was going to be fun.

My first year of deer hunting in 1969 was a combination of excitement and a lot of confusion. I had to ask myself, where is the fun? I had been told it would happen. That first year the season was later than usual, colder than usual and the Minnesota deer count was down. That meant most hunting parties would harvest fewer whitetail deer.

The clothing I used for this first hunt was all cotton except for my socks, they were wool. My long underwear, my skivvies, my pants, my red jacket and gloves were all cotton. I soon found that cotton is an especially good conductor of the cold. It is poor for insulating the body from the cold. My boots were rubber boots. Like the ones you would wear to keep your feet dry. Even with the wool socks they were of little use in the cold of winter.

I was confused, when was the fun going to start? Did the fun ever start in this iceberg climate?

I had been told all my life how great deer hunting and camp life was. I was very cold. On top of the cold that first day nobody even saw a deer. I was still waiting for the fun of deer hunting. I was still waiting for some fun and excitement.

The first morning we left camp at 6:30 am. Our walk to our stands took 20 to 30 minutes. Dad found a stand for me. It was a plank nailed to a tree limb. I guess I never had been told what constituted a stand. A board nailed to a tree was not my idea of a stand.

Dad told me to sit there and watch for deer. Dad explained how important it was to stay on stand. Dad told me; many times people have gotten off their stands and lost a chance to harvest a deer. My instructions were not to move until somebody came to get me. There I was with my cold butt sitting on a cold board.

My feet were getting colder by the minute. My hands were freezing. Now I was failing to see how anything about deer hunting could be fun, great and/or exciting. My hunting dreams had taken a 180 degree turnaround. The score for that morning was deer none, fun and excitement zero/cold and miserable ten.

Finally Dad came by and we trudged back to the cabin. At the cabin everybody was complaining about the cold and lack of deer in the area.

One of the guys who did the cooking had dinner ready for us. We were eating by 6 PM. By now I was starting to warm up and so was everybody else. Now the complaining was being replaced by "can you top this" stories.

The camp mood was swinging from complaining about the weather to reminiscing about the good hunts several years ago. At least camp life was somewhat enjoyable.

About 8 pm one of the old guys yelled, lights out. It was only 8 pm; nobody goes to bed at 8 pm. Wrong, at deer camp they do. The next morning I found out why. They go to bed at 8 pm and get up at 4 am in the morning. It always took over two hours for everybody to eat, make sure their bunk would air out and then get dressed and ready to walk out to their stand. Maybe they could sleep a little longer, I thought, but "tradition" prevailed; four AM was it.

The second evening I was ready to go to bed at 8 pm. From 4 am to 8 pm was a long day of work. You may not think trying to stay warm is not work but it is.

The trip into the deer camp that Friday was also a big part of my first deer hunting experience. The road in was muddy and we had to leave our cars out by the minimum maintenance road. At night taking a chance on getting stuck was not an option. The mud holes were obstacles Dad and the others did not want to tackle at night.

Their reluctance to drive further meant we had a mile and a half hike to reach camp. The good part of what was happening was the availability of Dad's new Swamp Buggy. We were able to load it with much of the bulky and heavy gear we had with us.

Dad drove, we walked. The pecking order concept was in full bloom. The walk would not have been so bad except it was cold; I had to carry a pack and my rifle. They all said, look at it this way; we got all the way to the logging road. If we would have stopped at the beginning of the minimum maintenance road, it would have been another mile of walking. I am not sure that their reasoning made me feel any better about the cold and the long hike in the dark that was facing us that night.

The Swamp Buggy was a track style machine. Dad and Doug had made it several years earlier. It was a great machine for traveling over the muddy roads to and from camp. Dad had secured an old 60 h p V-8 Ford engine that he used for the Swamp Buggy's power.

As I said earlier it was a great machine. Maybe that was where the word "great" came into deer hunting. So far nothing else had been as "great" as I had expected it to be. As great as the Swamp Buggy was it did have limitations. We still had to carry in packs and on our backs with some of the food and personal gear needed in camp.

After I had walked a mile I spotted the glow of a Coleman lantern through the pines. It was a welcome sight. It meant, soon I would be able to shed my pack and start to warm up.

I barely shed my pack so I could warm up before the pecking order again came into play. Several of us younger hunters had to unload the Swamp Buggy and carry our supplies into the cabin.

The older guys who were already warmed up would put the gear, food, and supplies away. The ones we had just carried into the shack on our backs. We also had to carry into the shack the food, equipment and supplies that were hauled to our camp in the Swamp Buggy.

The equipment, supplies and food were finally put away. I then was allowed to worry about my own gear. I was at the bottom of the pecking order. I did get to choose a place to call my bunk. I could take the available upper bunk or I could sleep on a mat in the old fish house. One place was heated the other was not.

For a cold first time deer hunter the choice was easy. I chose the upper bunk in a three high bunk system.

The top bunk and I got along very nicely. It was nice until someone stoked the fire and got the cabin very warm. I soon found out what the problem with the upper bunk would be. Because of the wood stoves heat you didn't need blankets. Then two hours later, after the fire in the wood stove died down, you needed all the blankets you could get.

Here I was taking the covers off me, then trying to find them so I could cover up again. It was just another problem I had not heard about prior to arriving at the deer camp.

The upper bunk reminded me of our sauna. You get all warmed up, start to sweat and then run outside and jump in a cold lake. I found that I had my own personal sweatbox in that top bunk. I did not need a sauna.

The cabin lighting system relied on a small gas light that was screwed into an overhead 2 by 4. It had a direct line to our propane system that also provided fuel for our cook stove. It worked but was inadequate and was supplemented with one or two Coleman lanterns.

That first hunt still left me confused. Everything was work, trying to keep warm and/or hoping things would get better. One glimmer of hope I found in the stories the older hunters told each evening. They would always raise my spirits and rekindle my deer hunting dreams. My dreams of fun, excitement and of harvesting a deer with the Lean-To-Boys were always rekindled by their stories.

After that first year or two I found my niche. I started to enjoy deer hunting and camp life. On one work weekend we were cutting wood for our camp when we discovered how easy it was to split the Cedar rounds into shingles. My uncle Leon, who was a machinist, made a special wedge for splitting the rounds into shingles. It worked very well.

The next weekend we split the rounds, ones we had saved just for the project, into a big pile of shingles. The next weekend or two, again on work parties, we sided the shack with our new Cedar shingles. They dressed the shack up and added a nice touch to its appearance.

As time and more hunting seasons piled up I was developing my own stories of hunting deer. I soon realized, the cold, staying warm, the work, and the stories are as much a part of deer hunting as actually harvesting a deer.

Deer hunting has become for me the greatest sport of them all. I recommend hunting to all my friends. It offers all of us great opportunities for enjoyment of the outdoors.

Now my wife, son and I hunt in a camp near the Lean-To-Boys camp. We do share with the LTB's their big Friday night steak fry. It is held at their camp on the night before the season opener. We also drop in during the evening of the first or second day to compare notes on how well everybody is doing, or on occasion, how well we all are not doing.

Our satellite camps story, my wife's successes and the family hunting experiences are the making of another chapter for another book. Until then, I wish you good hunting.

This is the dressed up 1st hunting cabin with its Cedar Shakes. When this picture was taken the fish house in front was long gone.

Chapter 18

BIGFORK BEAR HUNTING

Charlie Turnbull

My friends and I knew there were bears in Itasca County. In fact, we knew there were a lot of black bears. For years, we did not hunt them. I am not sure why we passed up bear hunting.

They weren't protected back in the 1950s and 1960s. We always said, during the firearms deer season, we would take one if we had the chance. It just wasn't something that caught our attention.

Once in the early 1960s, we had a new snow, and damned if we did not run across a fresh bear track. It was the day before the opening of the deer season.

We are not allowed to hunt with legal firearms several days prior to the deer season opener. Because of that law, Junior and I said we would follow the bear track in the morning.

That night, we felt pretty certain we could track and find that bear. We did not take into account the weather. It snowed heavily that night. The tracks were well covered up the next morning. We were disappointed that we could not follow up on that bear.

Several years later, the State of Minnesota put bears on the list for hunting, and set limits on their harvest. The State also charges prospective bear hunters a fee to enter a "lottery" to obtain the right, if drawn, to buy a license. Shortly after that, we seriously started thinking about bear hunting.

Jim was the first one in our party to actually go bear hunting. He built a stand on his acreage and actually harvested one back in the 1970s.

Jim also harvested a cinnamon bear. It is a black bear, but one with a mutation that is cinnamon-colored. Jim's success got us motivated, and we started hunting and harvesting black bears.

One year, Jim used cake frosting for bait. He stored part of it in the fish house during the hunt. During the day, the bear chose not come to his bait. The bear, one night, came to the fish house to check out the sweet smelling frosting. It smelled so good he tore a hole in the side of the fish house. The bear then carried off Jim's five-gallon pail of a very sweet-smelling frosting. The next morning when Jim surveyed what the racket in the night was all about, he found out. To add insult to injury the bear only went 30-40 yards away and had a "cake frosting feast." All Jim had is an empty five-gallon container and no bear that season.

In 1982, I finally took up bear hunting. I started out two weeks before the season opener, which is the first of September. That always gives us an early hunt over the three-day Labor Day weekend.

That first scouting visit in mid-August was to set up a stand and to start the 'baiting' procedure near the stand. The second visit was to re-bait the area where the stand was located.

I knew a bear was feeding in the area when I saw my bait station had been hit. The bait was set up so that the only animal that could reach it would be a bear. The bear had torn the area up where the bait had dripped, or after he spilled it onto the ground as he was feasting on the bait. For me, that was encouraging. Hopefully, he would be around the next week when I returned to actually start my bear hunting adventures.

On Labor Day week end, I arrived at Bigfork ready to go. This was a new adventure for me, and I had no idea of what to expect or what would happen if I did see a bear.

My stand looked good. It was a platform about four foot square, six feet off the ground, with an appliance box sitting on top of it. I also had a pail to sit on. The big appliance boxes are a natural for keeping your movements hidden. I have found that the bigger appliance boxes also do a good job of keeping your scent contained. Your scent does not blow downwind as readily when you are seated in one. With your body surrounded by cardboard, and with only your head showing, the wind has little chance of carrying your scent.

I went to my stand around 3 pm on that first Saturday in September. I crawled up the ladder, took my seat on the five-gallon pail and waited. I soon found out that September hunting is easier than cold November hunts. But it is not a cake walk. Minnesota's cold weather is one thing to deal with, and we have mastered it fairly well. In the winter, we just take a lot of heating equipment to our stands to stay warm. Although September does not require as much equipment as we need in the winter, it has its own special problems.

September goes out of its way to provides us with the very hungry "Minnesota Mosquito." One time, I even had to use a hat with netting that came down to my shoulders to combat the flying buggers. It worked, but it was a nuisance.

The hours went by from 3 to 4 pm and so on till 7 pm. As the sun was setting in the west, it was definitely starting to cool down. About 7:30 p.m., I was wondering if my first attempt would be a bust. On that first day on my bear stand, I had no idea as to when or what might happen. Ten minutes later I saw my first bear at Bigfork. For me, it was a pleasant surprise to see her. She crawled silently on all fours into my shooting lane. As she moved ahead very quietly toward the bait station, it was hard to guess her size. She was not a little bear, but it was hard to really know how big she really was. I took the shot and she dropped in her tracks.

I waited for about fifteen minutes before I exited the stand. I was not sure how close I could get to that bear and still be safe. I finally walked up to her and nudged her with my rifle; she did not move. I finally decided she was dead; I could start dressing her out.

By this time the sun had settled, and I had several hours of work ahead of me. I felt good about my first time on a bear hunt. The work that needed to be done just went with the thrill of being successful on my first day of bear hunting. One of our hunters showed up and we skinned her in the light from a Coleman lantern.

When that was done we hung the meat to cool in the night air. The next day, we packed the meat for the trip home.

We estimated that the bear I shot to be about 180 to 200 pounds. She was a nice bear, but not a monster. The meat was very delicious and the hide made a good "bear-skin rug."

Several years later my daughter, Terry harvested one. She was using the same stand that I had built and used for my first bear.

Bear stands and deer stands are basically similar if not the same. The difference is in the selected location for them. With deer you really have to make sure they are using the trails you are covering. With bears, you want to be in the area where bears are located. With their great sense of smell, they will come to the bait if they are anywhere near and interested in a free lunch.

The above makes it sound like all you have to do is put the bait out and "bingo" you're a successful bear hunter. They don't always come to bait. Blueberries, hazel nuts, acorns and other natural foods may be more to their liking from time to time.

Another factor is the time of day they are feeding. We have been on stands until shooting hours end and come back in the early morning hours only to find the bear came during the night time hours.

A "good bear bait" depends on several factors. The first, in my opinion, is what the bears are feeding on in the area to be hunted. Sometimes, there may not be bait that is best, if their food supply is abundant. So what is the answer to "what is the best bear bait"? The answer, "it depends".

I know the above is not really a good answer. All I can do is share with you some recipes that have worked for us at different times.

<u>Recipe #1.</u> A cheap dry dog food, cooking oil, sugar and anise flavoring mixed together works fairly well. The dog food gives you some bulk, and it is made out of grains and other products that are edible.

The oil is good in and of itself, and it binds the sugar to the dog food. The sugar adds flavor that the bears seem to like. The anise flavoring is used as a scent sender; the anise smell carries a long way.

Recipe #2. Again, dog food and used restaurant cooking oils mixed together can be good. The oils the restaurants give you have the flavors of the meat and fish cooked into them.

Make sure the restaurants cooking oils are not rancid. I had some once and I think it tainted the flavor of the bear. It is like eating a Merganser duck. They taste like fish because they eat fish. I think that happened with my second bear. He ate the rancid bait over a two-week period and his meat had acquired an off-taste.

Recipe #3. Day old bread and/or sweet rolls that are thrown out by bakeries can usually be purchased at a reasonable price. Couple the bread with the other ingredients: sugar, anise and cooking oil.

I was able to secure sweetened cereal once that worked. Meat scraps work, but they need to be cooked. I have heard that a honey pot works, but it needs to be heated to get the best aroma floating through the woods. Fruits and vegetables that a super market is tossing can be good too.

Jim even used cake frosting that a baker had made. It had been mixed wrong and the flavor was not correct. The bears liked it because it was made of sugar and oil; it was sweet and they go for that.

Something like anise flavoring is needed if the bait does not have its own fragrance to float over the countryside. The best rule of thumb is "If I would like it, the bear probably will, too."

Bear was new to our diet that first winter. My wife, Marlene, learned how to prepare it, and the family enjoyed it. She took a big bowl of Bear Stew to work one day to share it with the other realtors; some of them turned up their noses, but some tried it. They liked it and were always asking when she would bring Bear Stew to work again.

Others in our hunting party also have had success in hunting bear. The above stories are just a few examples of what the Lean-To-Boys have done as bear hunters.

We do have a few regrets after all the fun and work we have had over the last 35 years. Our primary regret is, why did it take so long to get started bear hunting?

Notes: Historical notes, on Minnesota black bear hunting, provided by the MN. Department of Natural Resources.

1. 1917, bear protected Mar.1-Oct.15; Steel traps for bear outlawed.
2. 1923, bear season set Oct.15-Jan.1.
3. 1927, bear given big-game status, big-game license required.
4. 1931, bear season open during deer season, and a spring season was established.
5. 1943, protection for black bear removed.
6. 1945, bounty for bear authorized.
7. 1954, three counties reestablished protection of bear.
8. 1971, bear season reestablished, 09/18-10/31, cubs protected, license fee $5.00.
9. 1982, lottery system for bear licenses established.

Other minor changes were made in fees and several other related areas. Since 1982, there have not been any major changes.

Chapter 19

THE BUCK KING

Punky has been hunting with the Lean-To-Boys since 1954. That year, he hunted with his dad and brother Leon. His dad, Clarence, was one of the original Lean-To-Boys.

At first, Punky was not a good shot. Even though he had served in the Marine Corps, and they put a lot of emphasis on shooting ability, he was still only an average shot. His brother, Junior, who is an expert rifleman, found this a bit frustrating.

Some years are not only good, they are superb. In 1962, we harvested eight deer for six hunters. We were able to do that because, in Minnesota, you can "Party Hunt." When another party was doing poorly, we offered to help them fill their tags. If they thought that was a good idea, we would be able to join their party. They did, and we filled two of their tags.

That year, Punky had his best year deer hunting. How he became the camp's "Buck King" is legendary. His hunting stories and his thoughts on deer hunting are found in this chapter.

Chapter 19
The Buck King
Punky Sjodin.
#1, Becoming 'The Buck King'

I am a straight shooter. I had my Marine Corps rifle training along with my families and Lean-To-Boys hunting experiences. My poor shooting told me I wasn't doing very well when it came to harvesting deer. I discussed this with my brother Junior. He said, "Punky, I am going to buy a scope for your rifle." He did, since that time I started hitting all my shots. I went from poor to good in my shooting.

Soon after I started using my rifle with the scope on it I became the "Buck King" in the Lean-To-Boys' Camp. They cannot take my crown away. I earned it in 1962, the year I harvested five fully antlered buck deer. So far no one has come close to my record.

As I said before no one in camp can take my crown a way. To do so would require them to harvest six fully antlered buck deer. Even if they came close I would just have to go out and raise the stakes.

So far it has not been necessary to even worry about it. My challenge to the Lean-To-Boys is for them to try and beat my record. If they can they have to do it within the rifle season.

Archery hunting does not count. They have over three months to hunt. The rifle season only allows a hunter 9 to16 days of hunting.

My record was established in 1962. I have been waiting for decades for someone to challenge me. So far, there have been no viable challengers. As I said before if someone comes close, let me know. I'll go out and up the ante so that I may retain my camps "Buck King" crown.

#2, the Butterscotch Bear

The best or at least most interesting bear hunt I have ever been on happened in 1986. I was hunting with Charlie's daughter, Terry. We were using the Lean-To-Boy's cabin that Labor Day weekend.

She had hunted deer in the late 70s with her twin sister Mary, brother and dad, Charlie, in the Bigfork area. Because girls and women do not hunt the first weekend in the Lean-To-Boys camp, Charlie set up a camp for his family at the creek.

They hunted from that location for 3 or 4 years. During those hunts at Bigfork, with family members, Terry harvested a fork horn buck. It was the only one harvested by 17 hunters in the two camps that year's opening day.

Somehow Charlie talked Terry into applying for and securing a bear permit in 1986. She was a senior at Iowa State University and could only devote the Labor Day weekend to bear hunting. They arrived in our camp just before dark on Friday. She was ready to go the next morning.

Saturday morning Terry and I headed out to our stands. Even though it was the first Saturday in September it was still chilly in the morning. We agreed to return to camp around 10 AM. We could at that time have a late breakfast.

It also gave us a chance to regroup and to determine any hunting changes we might want to make. She said she needed some warm socks. She forgot her socks when she left Iowa State the day before.

Charlie was not hunting but he did take the time to have our breakfast ready when we came in around 10 am. He also had the cabin picked up and ready for us.

Neither one of us had seen a bear. We discussed what to do for the evening hunt. We decided to continue to use our same stands that evening. There was no real reason not to use them.

While we were on our stands that morning Charlie took some of our sloppy bear bait and rubbed it on a tree that was near the cabin. The tree was 30 yards east of our cabins back door.

As we were sitting there eating and evaluating our next move Charlie would look out every 20 or 30 minutes to check the tree with bait smeared on it. It was his hope a bear might smell the bait on the tree and show up in camp.

This went on for about an hour and a half. After breakfast, close to 11:30 AM, I poked my head out the door to check on the bait. I could not believe it. There was a big black bear licking the tree where the bait was smeared on the tree.

You wouldn't believe the excitement at that moment. Terry and I started scrambling for our rifles and shells. I was able to get my rifle loaded and stepped outside the door. In that way I was able to get a good clean shot.

With Terry and Charlie hanging out the back door watching I took a shot. The bear ran a short distance and fell. Once you harvest a bear that is when the work begins. We had several hours of work ahead of us.

The bear I harvested was approximately 200 pounds. Because the bear's hide is such a good insulator, it is important when field dressing the bear, to remove it as soon as possible. In that way the meat starts to cool and does not turn sour.

By placing a canvas on the ground we were able to field dress the bear and keep the meat clean. Once this was done we were able to hang the meat so it could continue cooling. After a couple of hours of work we were able to sit down and relax.

That experience of harvesting a bear right outside of our cabin and the excitement of it was only the first half of this best and interesting bear hunt. Our initial plan was to go out to our stands at 4:30 PM.

Charlie said that bear proved one thing, they are "up and about" and Terry should get back on her stand as soon as possible. Charlie helped Terry get ready to go out to her stand. He also prepared another bait bag to bring to her stand.

She grabbed several big handfuls of butterscotch candies to suck on while sitting in her stand. Charlie tied the sack of bait on the back of his "Jim Dandy" lawn tractor and they headed out to her stand. She was on stand closer to 3:00 PM, instead of 4:30.

After dropping her off at the stand Charlie, with the bait bag dragging behind his "Jim Dandy", took off for town to buy her warm socks. Charlie wanted her to stay on her stand, to do that Terry needed a pair of warm socks.

He drove to town and purchased several pairs for her and delivered them to her. Latter she said they really helped her stay warm and on the stand.

After dropping the socks off he returned to the cabin to wait. Not much for him to do at that point except tidy up the cabin.

This is probably a great place to describe Terry's stand. You have to picture three trees forming a triangle, about 4 feet apart, with 2x4 cross pieces nailed to them. The cross pieces provided the structure for the boards that formed the platform. With three trees a 2x4 was used for the fourth leg. Then Charlie put a large appliance box on top of the platform. The platform was only 6 feet above the ground. With the appliance box on the platform and the front of it cut to form a make shift door you now have a stand with cardboard sides to sit in. A ladder and chair made it complete.

The beauty of this was the box gave you 36 inch sides all around. It shielded any small movements you made, ones a bear might see and then shy away from your stand. The sides of the box also aided in confining your body smells and kept them from drifting down wind and alerting the bear to a potential danger. It was a good stand and had proven its worth several years earlier when Charlie harvested a bear from it.

When Charlie got back to camp he reported that Terry had not seen a bear while he was in town. She was staying warm and the socks would help.

She was also enjoying the butterscotch candies. Charlie knew this because he saw all the butterscotch candy wrappers on the ground by her stand.

She was sure, with the new socks, staying warm would be no problem. I went out to the area by my stand to see if anything was happening out that way. If anything was happening it might be a good place for Terry on Sunday.

It was starting to get late in the afternoon and I was still checking out my bear stand and the area around it. I heard a shot to the west of me. I didn't think anybody else was hunting in the area. It had to be Terry's shot I heard.

I headed back to the cabin to tell Charlie. By the time we left the cabin and were heading toward Terry's stand we had a rapidly setting sun. Day light was waning.

We were heading toward her stand and making really good time. About two thirds of the way there we ran into Terry trucking her way up the logging road. She was looking for help.

Our first question was did you shoot? She said yes, but added, "I think I got one." That answered what would have been our next question.

She also said she wasn't comfortable looking in the tall grass for a bear that may be wounded. She was real glad to have the two of us heading her way and ready to help.

When we got to her stand she showed us where she had taken the shot. She said, after the shot the bear disappeared. "I think I got it, but it's in tall grass and I don't plan to go out there and check by myself."

She had a rifle and I had mine, Charlie had a flashlight. Terry wasn't sure if a flashlight was good protection if the bear was still alive.

As we were walking through the tall grass we were having trouble even finding where the bear had been, let alone finding the bear. Charlie kept looking with the flashlight. Even though his daughter thought that the flashlight was a poor idea it worked out to our advantage.

With the flashlight he was able to find the bear lying dead in a beaver run. That area had previously been flooded and the beaver had made runs under the ice. With the ice and water drawn the beaver runs were little troughs or trenches throughout the grassy area.

Terry explained how she had been sitting in her stand and had been hearing the grunting and snorting of a bear, or some animal, one that was fairly close. She could never see it until she looked straight down the right side of her card board box.

That was when she first saw the black rear end of the bear. It was crawling right under her stand.

When they saw each other, both jumped. The bear jumped and disappeared into the woods. Terry said she was really disappointed at that time.

As luck would have it the bear reappeared out in a grassy meadow. She then was able to harvest her bear.

I have named that experience, the Butterscotch Bear Hunt. After all, that bear enjoyed smelling the butterscotch wrappers. The wrappers Terry had so casually been throwing over the side of her appliance box stand.

#3, the Drive of the Green Stamp Brigade

There was a time in the late 1960s when the Holiday gas station gave out green stamps. When you filled a booklet the Holiday gas station would redeem them for the merchandise they sold.

My buddy Bob and I purchased a lot of gas and other merchandise from Holiday gas stations. We always had several books that we were filling and eventually turning in for merchandise at their stations.

We were on our way to our deer hunting camp at Bigfork. We had just purchased gas. As we were paying for it when we noticed the Holiday station had orange colored plastic ponchos for sale.

The State of Minnesota had just recently gone from red to blaze orange as the color required for deer hunting. For one book of stamps we could purchase one of the ponchos.

We now had a way to stay dry and at the same time have orange around us when we were sitting or walking. These ponchos were just what the doctor ordered.

When we got to Camp we found out most of the other guys had seen the same ponchos on their way up to Bigfork. Everybody in camp was prepared for wet weather.

As fate would have it Sunday morning, the second day of the season, it was raining. We were prepared. We broke out our new water repelling ponchos. These ponchos were those pocket-sized ones that folded into a 3" x 5" package about ½" thick. Obviously the plastic was not very heavy, it was however orange in color and we would be able to stay dry.

Mid-morning we decided to make a drive through a wooded area. We needed to move the deer. Soon a drive was organized so we could start moving the deer. Up to that point things were fairly slow. We organized the drive. Two of us found places to stand to watch for deer if they moved out of the area we were driving.

The four guys who were doing the driving had to walk around the area and position themselves to make the drive. We figured it would take about 30 minutes to walk around the area and get on the other side of the woods. The two of us on stand would have to wait and be ready.

The two of us who were on stand had to be ready, because, the deer would be moving as they are walking or possibly leaping across the logging road. Our chance for a shot would be short at best.

We were in place, but nothing was happening. After about forty five minutes I saw the first driver. He had walked out onto the logging road. He was a real spectacle draped in a shredded orange poncho. Then a second driver stepped out, he had the same rag/tag appearance as the first one. The third one only had a small piece of the poncho wrapped around his neck. When the fourth driver appeared he had orange cuffs on his two wrists.

All in all they were a sight to behold. The lightweight, inexpensive, orange colored and really cheap ponchos were a waste of our green stamp books.

The next day I walked through the same wooded area that the drivers had walked through. The woods were decorated with blaze orange poncho fragments. I decided right then and there yesterday's drive was to be called the Drive of the Green Stamp Brigade.

#4, Forget the Doe

I was so wrapped up in shooting bucks I passed up shooting a doe. I saw her moving toward the survey line east of my fender stand. I also caught the movement of a second deer following her. I knew we were in the rutting season and the second deer could be a buck.

When the doe walked through the survey line I did not take a shot. I was waiting for the second deer. I was right the second deer was a buck. My shot was true and I had my buck. Waiting for the second deer to enter the survey line paid off.

When I got back to camp I told the story of how I was able to get a shot at the buck. I thought I had done a pretty good job of hunting that morning. The other guys gave me a bunch of crap about passing up on the doe.

They thought I should have taken the doe first and then, they were sure, the buck would have stopped to look. In that way they thought I could've had two deer. Who knows, all I know is I had my buck no matter what they thought.

#5, Let others do the work

Twice I have had other hunters through their actions push deer to me. One time I was sitting on a stump west of our camp. Two hunters were off in the distance walking through a large grassy area. I kept watching them until I saw a doe stand up.

The doe moved a few yards in my direction and looked over her shoulder toward the other hunters. She did this several times and shortly she was within my range for a shot. I dropped the doe in her tracks.

The other hunters who were with the Smith party came running up to me. They were yelling, you shot our deer, you shot our deer. I told them that we would go and take a look.

If the deer has two bullet holes or has their name written on it someplace then it would be their deer. Amazingly it only had one bullet hole and I could not find their name written on it. I thanked them for driving a nice deer to me.

The second time I had someone spook a deer in my direction I was sitting at the rock stand. Another party had a hunting camp about 400 yards behind me. They have a shack in their camp they call Stallag 13. Evidently they were World War II veterans and liked the Stallag 13 name for their camp.

That morning I had walked out to my stand fairly early. I was sitting there when all of a sudden the quietness of the morning was broken. The Stallag 13 party had just gotten up and started their generator.

A nice buck was coming my way and was exiting himself from the noise of their camp. The buck appeared to be sneaking away from them. It was all to my advantage, I now had another buck to talk about.

Sometimes it's just better to let someone else do the work. It sure worked out that way for me. There is only one thing to say, thank you.

#6, Is it luck or is it skill?

Twice I harvested a deer for two other Lean-To-Boys hunters. One was Vince the other was Paul. They both wanted to head home with a deer. So far their hunting did not yield one. Each time I told them I would go out and harvest them a doe.

Sure enough both times I was back within the hour with the doe I had promised. Both of them claimed I was just "lucky."

Punky "you sure are lucky" is what I heard from both of them. No way, I told them. I asked Vince if he ever listened to his dad about hunting. He claimed he did, so I asked him what Charlie says about luck.

He thought for a moment or two then said, "My dad says deer hunting is 80 to 90% skill and 10 to 20% luck. I told Vince "right on" and your dad is correct. Deer hunting is 80 to 90% skill. Vince, I don't want you to ever forget it.

Work on your hunting skills and you will start harvesting more game. Your skills include shooting ability, tracking big game, knowing your hunting area, pre-scouting and then the placement of your stand where the deer travel.

If a hunter builds his skills as a hunter he will be successful. As I indicated above I will continue to rely on my skills. When I get "Lucky" that is "OK" too.

Remember, if I have to, as the camps 'Buck King' I will defend my crown. While I am waiting for a challenger I just might go out and improve upon my record. After all, others work at raising their records. I should too.

In closing I want to wish each of you good hunting and good eating.

Chapter 20

TERRY AND HER BEAR

Punky, Charlie, Terry and their two black bears

Terry told her Bear Story at our family's Thanksgiving get together one year. Her Aunt Helene Turnbull recorded and taped it while she told it. We have viewed it many times and have shared it with our friends, and now we have put it on a DVD. Terry definitely remembered the events involved in the hunt and has told the story well. For this book, we have had it transcribed from her video for everybody's enjoyment.

Chapter 20
Terry and her Bear
Terry Turnbull Leadabrand

One Thanksgiving my Mother, Father, Cousins and Nieces were sitting around my sister Char's Family Room when my Dad asked me to tell my bear hunting story. The way he said it was like this--- 'Somebody ask her to tell the story of the Bear that had to wake her up to shoot it.' That got a big laugh out of everybody.

Then Mom piped in, "---Hey Terry, tell them about it, tell them how at first the bear had to sign a white sheet of paper or something, tell us how it really happened." That got a few more laughs going. At that point I said, 'All right Dad' and I proceeded to tell the story.

Well, it all started in the spring of 1988; sometime in April or May just before I was getting done with school at Iowa State University. As I remember, it was a warm and sunny afternoon when I pulled a thick letter from the mailbox it was addressed to me from my Dad. Curiously I opened up the envelope and found Dad's cryptic note.

My Dad never sent long explicit letters. This was no exception, it read, 'Sign this, Dad.' That was it. That's all he wrote. Perplexed I looked at the accompanying documents and it was a lottery application for a Minnesota Bear Hunting Permit.

Smirking, I said to myself, 'Right, me going bear hunting! My twin sister, Mary, would never do this.' I wasn't even sure I ever wanted to go bear hunting. However, I knew it would make Dad happy if I applied. Besides the hunting would be on a holiday weekend, and, so I figured I wouldn't even get the permit. Nevertheless I signed my name on the dotted line, send it in and then didn't give it another thought.

At semester end I returned to our lake home just outside of Faribault, Minnesota for a couple of days before heading west to my summer internship. Being Dad and all, the first thing he said to me when I arrived home was, 'Did you get your bear hunt application'? I nodded affirmatively. Followed by did you sign it and send it in, the bear permit?' I responded with a simple 'Yeah' and Dad beamed.

A couple of days later I took off for Idaho.

That summer while I was interning in Idaho my Mom and Dad came to Pocatello for a visit, it was late in July. They were celebrating their 35th wedding anniversary. After our welcoming hugs and kisses dad informed me that I got a Bear Permit! He said, "And we are going bear hunting Labor Day weekend!" Somewhat sarcastically I responded "GREAT, JUST WHAT I WANTED TO DO Labor Day Weekend!"

In mid-August I returned to the Midwest to finish my last semester at Iowa State University. Coursework always started a few days before Labor Day.

I loved Labor Day weekend at Iowa State. There were so many parties, social events to attend and it is an idyllic time to catch up on summer happenings, but this year... I was going Bear Hunting.

As Labor Day weekend approaches, Dad is calling and asking, "Okay, how soon, can you get out of school?" I replied, "Well, I have class until 11 o'clock, I can leave after that. But, it will probably be more like 11:30 or 12, because I got to, you know, ride the bus home and get my car packed and stuff.'

Dad says, "'you've got to get all packed up the night before, and can't you drive to campus? Can't you leave any sooner? ... "Well okay", I replied.

Per Dad's request, I got all packed up the night before and drove to campus. I left immediately after class about 11-ish driving the three hours north.

I got into Faribault, Minnesota about 2 PM. While growing up my mom and dad were seldom home for a long time. So I drove into town to my parent's real estate company. I stopped at the office and said 'Hi, where's Dad?' And Moms like, 'Oh, he is waiting for you out of the house.' I called Dad and asked him where we are meeting?' Are we meeting here at the office or at home? He said, "God no, come to the house, we don't have much time."

So I jumped into my Chevy – Chevrolet and go be-bopping out to the lake house. We lived about 5 miles west of town on Cannon Lake it was 10 to 15 minute drive depending on if you were speeding or driving the limit. I was speeding and caught up to Dad about 2:15 PM. We removed my gear into his truck, grabbed some other supplies and to my amazement we were actually on the road about 2:30 PM.

We drove a quarter of the way around Cannon Lake and stopped. Surprised, I inquired what we are doing. Dad, with a knowing smile informs me, "We are getting stuff for the bear bait."

I soon learned bear bait is not complicated. It consists of 50 to 100 pounds of cheap dog food, 15 to 30 gallons of rancid stinky grease (from the local hamburger and French fry joint), and a half-dozen bottles of anise flavoring. Some over ripe fruit will superbly top it off.

After we obtained approximately 15 gallons of the stinky fryer grease we charged across the country side on back roads. We were heading north. From Faribault, Big Fork is a 5+ hour drive nearly straight north. However the Twin Cities are located between us and our destination.

Normally, Dad is a relatively a tame, mild driver and a real law abiding citizen. This day he was different, HE'S IN A BIG HURRY! I asked him, "What's the rush?" Excitedly he states, "We're trying to beat the rush-hour traffic in the Twin Cities. If we take Highway 18 we can take the back roads and maybe miss some of the traffic."

So we ended up speeding all the way to and from Anoka. Anoka is the town and area that was my Dad's old stomping grounds. While on Highway 18, Dad starts telling me about how the intersection in Anoka, about 25 years ago, when it was the main drag through town and any traffic coming east or west would go across or through the intersection.

Now we are racing north and we finally get up to this little hick town, a little south of Brainerd. About 45 minutes later when all of a sudden rumble, rumble, bump, bump and bump Dad yells "Shit I thought that might happen!"

Sure enough we had a flat tire. We pulled over to the edge of the road. Then, we get out to change the tire. *In true* Turnbull form, the spare tire is buried. To get at it we have to take out all of the bear bait, the smelly-smelly fruit and other crap.

Despite the flat, Dad announces, "But, I was prepared" while waving a shiny brand-new four-way wrench. I'm grateful for this, till the sucker broke. We cuss in unison "Shit!"

Then Dad and I rifled through his assorted tools. We luckily find and old tire wrench. However the shaft is short making the leverage LESS than ideal. Plus, the lug nuts are tight, dry and rusty. They are not budging. Both of us are pulling, still no movement. We improvise by jumping on this old little tire iron, practically stripping the bolts. We finally got them off, got the spare on and we're racing down the highway once again.

A flat tire kind of put us behind our schedule by about an hour. So we scrapped our plans of getting up to the cabin at 7 PM. My chance of getting out on the stand for the last half hour of hunting before Sunset was gone. Instead we slowed down and stopped in Grand Rapids for a fast food dinner at Hardee's.

Then we were back on the road. We finally got up to the cabin about 8:30 PM. Punky was there already, we gossiped late into the night, I'm telling Punky and Dad about this great summer I had at C.W. HOG and pretty soon I'm talking, like 'hello' and all I hear is snoring.

In reliving my exceptional summer, I was so wound up from talking that I couldn't fall asleep! I am like awake for several more hours into the morning. Finally I fall asleep. I wake up about 6:30 A. M. to a lot of commotion.

Dad's all excited and mumbling, like. "We overslept; we've got to get out there on those stands." So, at 7 AM we're out on our stands. Dad took me out to my stand on our three wheeled, all-terrain vehicle, and I stayed out there from 7:30 to 9 AM. By 9 AM I am cold and realizing how short I was of warm clothing. I thought Dad had packed everything we needed. Before we left I asked him if everything was packed, he said, "well yeah, I think I got most of it but check around and take what you need".

So I just assumed that my clothes and socks and so forth were in the truck. It was Labor Day weekend, and I was expecting nice, warm, timid and mild weather. But when we got out there, I was really flustered. I am out there with just tennis shoes and no socks my knees were knocking and I'm freezing and dying in this blustery weather. I'm, like, SNOW is imminent I just know that it is coming!

But I stayed out there from 7 to 9 freezing. At 9 AM Dad said I could come in, so, not a minute past, I'm off my stand and booking in because I was so cold. So it's Burr, Burr, and Burr. So I get back to the cabin and we're talking and Larry a friend of Dad and Punky, and Jim's son, was there.

He was gossiping with us and so forth, Punky stopped talking and stepped outside the back door. Dad and I were just sitting having coffee, chatting and I tried to warm up as I was making up my shopping lists. We didn't know how long this hunting trip was going to be so I was, like, I'm not going to sit there and starve. So, I was making out lists of all the cookies, candy and everything I wanted. By the time I had my list done I was ordering a half box of goodies plus the clothes Dad had to pick up in town, so I could stay warm and sit out on my stand.

As I said before, Punky stepped outside, but all of a sudden he came back in and he's like, "Oh shit! Charlie there's a bear out there!" And so everybody jumps up! And then were like "OKAY, OKAY. And they are all standing around the cabin going "okay!" It was a moment of clear confusion.

Dad and Punky are the only ones, who can see out the door, but we are all grabbing our guns and trying to load them the best we can and we're going okay, okay, okay!

Finally with Punky standing just outside the door and Dad looking out the door I hear Dad, like, "Punky shoot. Kill the bear!" Punky's like I'm trying, "JUST a minute, Charlie". Punky finally shoots and he gets his bear.

After the shot the bear ran off and headed into the woods. All of a sudden all you hear is this like moaning and more moaning and that's about it. And so were like, okay and so we, everybody, like okay, okay and they're all looking around to see if there's another bear around.

After a minute or two we all went trotting over there to see, and sure enough there is Punky's dead bear. We are all excited and stuff. Dad was like, "Well...Terry should be out on her stand." And so, this is about 11 AM. We take the time to field dress the bear and then we head back to the shack.

At the shack we take the time to clean up and then have something to eat. Dad said something about the bears must be eating around the clock. After all Punky's bear was out and about late in the morning. So at 1 PM Dad and I are again heading out to my stand.

After dropping me off at my stand Dad and Larry headed for town. They went to town and got me a hat and some wool socks and other stuff. Dad came back about 3 PM with some stuff and some candy and things to munch on.

And so I put on my socks and my hat and I'm all warm and comfortable. Also, I had borrowed Dad's boots so I could sit up there, I was pretty toasty.

About 3 PM Dad did another thing. He brought out more bear bait. So he's there talking to me while I am putting on the warm clothes he brought me. He's also, asking me if I saw anything and I'm telling him no, Nothing.

So he takes off, drops more bait and then takes off again. And I'm sitting out there, and it's two o'clock, three o'clock, I tried to read at least one chapter of Speech Communication for my college classes.

And, but every, I mean every second, I'm looking around and throughout the area. It is REALLY difficult to read as 'OH'. Every sound has to be checked and that makes my reading a difficult chore. I mean every second you're looking up and around. It's really difficult to read and all. Every noise is like, something is MOVING. You keep hoping that it's the bear coming.

My bear bait was directly in front of me. I also had bear bait off to my left. That was the one where dad had added the fresh bait. 4 PM rolls by… nothing has happened. 5 PM. rolls by and STILL nothing, as yet has happened. Now… I have been sitting there another three hours… it was 6 PM. I'm thinking to myself 'okay bear' you got two hours before its dark, you

Six PM rolls by. Pretty soon, "Mr. Bear you better come, we only have an hour and a half now, we're running out of time." So about a 6:45 I thought I had heard something, in fact it was a couple of times. And then I think I hear something else, and I'm looking around and I don't hear or see anything.

Pretty soon at 7:15, I looked at my watch, I heard something again. Now I was just like paying real close attention because I knew Dad had shot his bear about that time last year. Again, I thought I heard something. Now I'm really looking around and still nothing till about 7:30. I thought I heard something again, but like something sniffing at the ground. It was a snort, snorting sound. Just like you know someone is snoring or something like that. I'm still looking around and I don't see anything. All of a sudden, I heard it again. I think there's something down there and then the trees my stand was attached to started swaying. And there was no wind to cause that to happen.

"Oh my God there's something here… there's something happening." So I look over my right my shoulder and looking down, (I'm contained in this cardboard box so the bear can't see me) I see something BLACK right below me! I'm like 'Oh my God' there is a bear, its right underneath me… there really is." And so I leaned to the side just to make sure and sure enough there's this… GREAT BIG BLACK BUTT, right below me. Now I'm like 'oh my God this is TOO easy' …so I'm standing up… grabbing my gun and like 'this is going to be too easy…I can take my gun and shoot it straight down SIX feet below me.

Right a REAL challenge! And so all of a sudden I'm trying to grab my gun and while I'm grabbing my gun the bear puts his paws up on the front top two rungs of the ladder. The one Dad built for me to get up in the stand.

The bear is looking around and not paying attention kind of like sniffing the air. All afternoon I've been eating butterscotch candy and throwing the wrappers down on the ground.

The bear continued to sniff and he finally looks up and sees me. He gets startled and jumps back. And I jumped back too. Now my legs are like bouncing up and down… the adrenaline is going nuts and I'm like 'Oh my God'…as the bear goes bounding off through the trees

I'm terrified that my bear was gone. And I'm feeling all sorry for myself and I'm looking and I got my gun up to my shoulder looking through the scope and trying to see the bear. I'm checking underneath the evergreen trees that are about 20 feet away from me. You know I was thinking, 'Maybe I'll see it.' And so forth, I finally decided that I'm not going to see it. No other bear is going to show up right behind all that commotion!

So I sat down feeling all dejected and staring at this bait that's straight ahead of me. All of a sudden, as I'm sitting back and looking off to the left where the other 'bear buffet' was set up, and 'Oh my God' this great big black blob was there in the center of this tall grass field.

Again I'm like 'Oh my God that's my bear' it can't be anything else. Sure enough he stands up like Big Ben, so I stand up in my stand. I'm kind of standing a little bit sideways. My legs are bouncing up and down, you know like in the cartoons. You never believe them but it really happens. So then I feel like I'm jumping up and down and I'm trying to get a good stance so I can take a good shot.

I'm finally steadied, get the gun up to my shoulder and now have the bear in my sights. The crosshairs are perfect and I'm up there thinking and I don't remember if I took the safety off. Instead of just pulling the trigger to see if I have the thing on… no I had to take my head all the way around and look at it to see if the safety was off or on. Sure enough I saw it was off, I could have shot.

By now the bear is no longer standing up like Big Ben, he is down on all fours. I got my gun sighted again and I'm thinking 'Oh please don't go.' So with the gun back up in position and sighted in on the back of the bear's head and shoulders I pulled the trigger and shoot.

All of a sudden I hear a thud followed by the moaning; just like I heard earlier with Punks bear. And that was it. And so I'm like, 'Oh my God.' So I'm waiting around thinking, okay, all right… I'll just wait here…. there might be another one.

So I was just hanging out there and I'm waiting for another bear. None showed up and I'm, like, okay. Better if you go check on this bear because it was like 7:35 PM when I shot it or something close to that. It's going to get dark so I better go find this bear.

So I'm like trying to get out of my stand. Not easy to get out of this cardboard box plus my legs are shaking like crazy and I'm coming down this ladder with my gun and my legs are still shaking. So I go trotting over to the edge of this tall grass and I'm sitting, no I'm standing there with my gun.

I'm like thinking 'Oh my God what if I didn't hit it very well? What if I just wounded it? I didn't see it take off, but I just don't know where it went'. It happened so fast and I can just see this bear, this ravaging bear, it's like a grizzly, looking at me and attacking me. And I'm thinking NO WAY! I'm not going out and into the tall grass.

I went back and crawled up into my stand. I was sitting up there and I'm thinking, like, Dad and Punky might come by and then we'll 'all' go and find the bear.

And I'm sitting there and, I'm like, regaining my courage. I'm telling myself, 'You go deer hunting all the time. You can track the bear. You should do this, come on you can do this'. So once again I talk myself into getting out of my tree stand.

I'm shaking as I climb down the tree stand ladder. With my jittery legs I go over to the edge of the tall grass and start into it. I got like two steps further than where I was standing the first time. And I'm like no, no that's really okay. I'm a 'wimp' and very aware that I am not going in there any further.

And so I go back and start trotting off for the shack.-I'm on my way to get Punky and Dad. So I go walking and running down the logging road yelling, Dad, Punky, Dad!

As I'm heading for the cabin, all of a sudden, I hear the three wheeler and I'm like okay, cool, they are here. I'm like asking them, 'So did you hear me yelling?' and they answered no. Dad said, "No, Punky heard your shot, he came and got me, I didn't even hear it." All of us headed back to my stand after Punky told me to jump on the three wheeler.

There we're going into the tall grass to see if we could find the bear. I have my rifle; Punky has his rifle and my Dad's armed with his flashlight. Not quite dark yet but he is armed with a flashlight.

That worried me. But Dad is Dad and sometimes he's not overly careful. So we're going through the tall grass by the bait station. We're going through the grass and we're parting the grass with our rifles; I was ready to take a shot at a ravaging bear if I had to. WELL... it could be a very angry ravaging bear.

Punky asked, 'Where was the bear when you shot at it?' I was sure this was the right area. I said, 'Well in my sights it looked up really close, but this would probably be a good spot'. So we continued to look, Dad is still parting the tall grass looking for the bear.

He is shining the flashlight and all of a sudden he's like, 'Okay wait... wait a minute I think we got it'! And there, sure enough, is my bear lying in a gulley the beavers had created when the meadow was under water.

The first question was, is he dead? 'I don't know.' I said. So I poke he bear with my gun, I'm sure any minute now the bear is going to jump up and attack me, but no he's really dead.

We pulled him out of the gulley, through the grass and over to my stand. We field dressed him, cleaned up the mess and headed back to the cabin. At the cabin we hung him up, took his hide off, and had him opened up. By doing this he really cooled down that night.

The next day we broke camp and headed home with our two bears. On Labor Day 1988 I headed back to Iowa State University. That school year 1988/1989' I completed my degree in Therapeutic Recreation. Then I headed back to Idaho and my first professional position as a Recreation Therapist at CW HOG.

Authors Note: That's my bear story! But, my Dad claims, 'The bear had to wake me up to shoot it.' That's not entirely true. But it's hard to believe that I had a 200 pound bear less than 2 to 3 feet below my feet as I was sitting in my 'card board box' bear stand.

It was the experience of a life time and in the end I didn't even miss… missing, all the parties at I. S. U., that Labor Day weekend. I, in fact had a party. It was a bear hunting party; that hunt was more exciting and more rewarding than any other party could have been. Thanks Dad and Punky for making it happen.

Chapter 21

HUNTING, FRUSTRATION AND REDEMPTION

Our friend Jim joined our hunting camp in the early 1970s. We first met him in 1952, the first year we hunted the Bigfork area. Back then, Jim was a 17-18-year old kid out hunting with his old 44/40 rifle. He was staying at his abandoned house located on the family's 120-acre farm. The farm is located at the end of the minimum maintenance road.

We found out later that the old farmhouse had been empty for several years. Jim's mother had bought the 80-acre farm in 1944. She had remarried after that, and she and her new husband added another 40 acres. Jim lost his mother in 1949. With her death, Jim and his stepfather left the farm.

After Junior and I returned from military service, we again ran into Jim. He had formed his own hunting party, and they were staying in the old deteriorating farm house.

In some of our stories, the Smith hunting party is mentioned. For the most part, the Smith party hunted the open fields and woods on or near his 120 acres. The Lean-To-Boys' camp and hunting area was approximately a mile and a half east of the farm. The logging road to our camp actually traveled through the southeast 40 acres of the Smith Farm.

Jim dissolved the hunting party after years of his party's poor success and their lack of interest in keeping the house usable. We invited him to join our party. This worked out well for him and for us.

Jim had been a cook in the Army. It didn't take long for him to become the cook for our camp. His opening morning breakfast of SOS soon became a camp staple. His SOS recipe lasted for decades in the Lean-To-Boys' camp. SOS is still a staple, on opening morning, but, with the new cook taking over in 2009, the recipe changed a little bit.

Part of Jim's frustration years ago with his hunting party was the fact that they didn't want to help keep the house in good enough repair. The guys he hunted with wanted to hunt there but not to contribute to the upkeep needed or to help pay any taxes on the property. Eventually, Jim had enough. We invited him to join our party, and he did. The rest is history, and shows up in various ways in the stories found in this collection of memoirs.

In this chapter, Jim touches on his need to disband the Smith party, and his cooking and hunting as a member of the Lean-To-Boys' hunting camp.

Chapter 21
Hunting, Frustration and Redemption
Jim Smith

I have always loved hunting. As a kid living in the Bigfork area hunting and fishing were naturals. In the fall I could roam the woods and hunt ruff grouse. During the nine-day deer hunting season I had the farm to myself. During the other three seasons I could fish the Bigfork River and many of the nearby lakes. It was great being a kid and living on a farm just outside of Bigfork.

The farm was located at the end of a road that was designated by the Township as a "minimum maintenance road." Back in the 40's the school bus came all the way back and picked me up for school. It was a good life, at least for me.

Shortly after buying the 80 acre farm my mother remarried. She and my stepfather purchased an additional 40 acres. In 1949 when I was 15 years of age my life took a change, my Mom passed away.

It was over 50 years before we had my mother's probate settled. I was entitled to have the original eighty acres and one half of the forty acres. It must be noted that my stepfather remarried and raised another family. I have a stepbrother living on the south 20 acres. He too likes to hunt and fish.

The first deer I shot as a kid on the farm was in 1947. It was a buck. I shot it near the house, I was so proud and happy, and it was my first deer. Mom wasn't happy about that. She said, "Bucks are too tough." We ended up canning most of that deer. To me it didn't make any difference. After all I had been successful and for a kid of 14 that was pretty good.

Because the Big Fork River cuts through a corner of our land I did most of my fishing on the river. I remember catching a lot of Northern Pike and Muskies in the river. One day I caught a big musky; it must've been over 12 pounds and 30 inches long. It wasn't a world record but for me it was a nice fish.

After leaving the farm my chances for hunting dropped off. I would drive to the farm to hunt grouse and deer. I remember the first year I met some of the Lean-To-Boys. It was back in 1952. I had just graduated from high school that year and I was staying at the farm during the deer season.

I was walking down the logging roads about two miles east of the farm when all of a sudden somebody said, "Be careful with that rifle." It scared the hell out of me.

At first I didn't know where the command came from. I looked up and there was a guy up in a nearby tree. I found out later it was Junior's dad, Clarence. Later on I ran into Junior and Charlie. They were surprised somebody else was hunting two miles from the road.

I ended up being drafted and served two years cooking in the Army. When I returned home and started work I met a couple of guys who wanted to do some deer hunting. I invited them up to the farm to hunt with me.

This worked out pretty well for two or three years. We eventually needed to fix up the old farmhouse. It had been sitting empty for seven or eight years. We were using the house for our camp and shelter and we needed to fix it up. We needed a few windows repaired and a better wood stove for heat. Nobody was willing to pitch in and help.

We, the Smith Party, had been hunting for five or six years together. As a hunting party we never did real well. We would get one or two deer each year. The deer were there, we just couldn't hit them. Several times we got help filling our deer tags by having the Lean-To-Boys hunt with us. They shot several deer for us over a 3 or 4 year span.

I got tired of my party's lack of help and any interest in keeping the old farm house up. It needed some repair so we could continue living in it during the deer season. Because I had a growing friendship with the Lean-To-Boys and recently had been invited to join them I disbanded the Smith hunting party in 1970. I never have looked back since making that decision and move.

By joining their hunting party I was starting to have more fun hunting deer than I had had for a long time. Getting rid of the frustrations I had with my own party was a great decision. For me changing parties was a real opportunity, it was like a form of redemption and offered me a chance to relax, and again, enjoy hunting.

Hunting with people truly committed to deer hunting has been a high light of my life. Some fifty years later with a few more aches and pains I still get up in the morning and head out to my deer stand and I will as long as I can.

Chapter 22

THE LEAN-TO-BOYS TAKE UP ELK HUNTING IN IDAHO

Charlie Turnbull

In the early 1990s, three of us headed to Idaho for our first elk hunt. The two Steve's (Quade and Sjodin) and I started out four days before the September 15th season opener.

Steve Sjodin's Ford Ranger pickup truck was our means of transportation. Along the way, we rested and caught a few hours of sleep at a Montana rest stop. The trip took us two days to reach our designated point with Terry.

At the same time, my daughter Terry was traveling north from Pocatello, Idaho to hook up with us. Terry, at the time of this Elk Hunt, was a recent graduate of Iowa State University and was working in Pocatello, Idaho. She was working for a recreation program sponsored by Idaho State University. Idaho State University's recreation program is called "Cooperative Wilderness Handicapped Outdoor Group" (CW HOG). The agency provides challenging outdoor recreational opportunities for people with a variety of handicaps. At that time, Terry was a Recreation Therapist in the program.

We were able to meet up with her just south of Darby, Montana. It was at the junction of Montana highway 43 and US highway 93. From this point, we headed north to Connors, and then west out of Montana and into the Bitterroot Mountains. We soon were crossing over the Montana State line at 6,587 feet and through the Nez Perce Pass. Now, we were in the wilderness area of Idaho.

We were headed into the Idaho hunting area #17, located within the Selway Zone. The Selway River is the identifying feature in the zone. In addition to area #17, the Selway Zone consists of three other areas: 16a, 18 and 19.

The route we took into and through the Selway Zone was over the Nez Perce Trail. It is in the same area where the U.S. Army was unsuccessful in finding the Nez Perce Tribe and Chief Joseph, during their mission to do so in the late 1800s.

The Army, eventually, was successful in catching and corralling the tribe. It was, only, when the Nez Perce Tribe moved out of the Idaho Mountain's wilderness area and onto a flatter part of Montana and the Tribe stopped to camp at Big Hole, Montana

There was a short war between the two adversaries, after which the Army was finally able to complete its mission. A Federal Park at that location commemorates the significance of the campaign.

Since that trip, I have read the book <u>I Will Fight No More Forever</u>, which is an account of the search and encounter between the US Army and the Nez Perce Tribe. The book was written by Merrill D. Beal, and is available through Amazon.com. The book highlights the importance of Chief Joseph, and it is a good historical read about a proud tribe, their ordeals and the tribe's chief, Chief Joseph. By reading it, you will soon realize just how elusive people or animals can be in the wilderness and mountains of Idaho. We soon found out; finding elk in these same mountains can be just as daunting an experience. Especially, when people like us had no previous elk hunting experience.

The Selway Zone is a beautiful, mountainous and challenging part of the State of Idaho. The mountains are steep and rugged, and offer hunters and hikers a true test of their stamina and staying power.

The flow of the Selway River is very rapid and fast charging in its downhill trek to its confluence with the Clearwater River. In the spring, kayakers dream of making the Selway run. For them, the thrill is to master the river's "Class 5" challenges. The river's water is very cold all year long; in the spring, it has to be next-to-freezing, with no room for any errors in a kayaker's judgment.

Several miles after entering Idaho, we found ourselves driving alongside the Selway River. As we traveled further along the river, we soon passed by the U.S. Forest Ranger Station and its staff who service that area in the Bitterroots. We continued to drive along the river, looking for the road that would take us to our planned camping area. After we found the forest road and turned south, we soon crossed a bridge. Now, we were heading south and away from the Selway River.

The forest road that heads up to the area we planned to use for our camp was rougher than the one we used as we traveled alongside the river. It is the Forest Service road that eventually winds its way from the river on its way to Elk City, Idaho.

Along the way to our camping area, we drove through Kim Creek Campground. We then passed by the marked trail leading to the historically-significant Maggruder Massacre site.

We moved on up the forest road a few miles to our camp site at Lookout Point. The camping area is on the slopes of 7,000' Dead Top Mountain.

Only a few miles further up the road, Salmon Mountain looms up over 8,943 feet. At a lower elevation by 1,500 feet, on one of Salmon Mountains' slopes, you will find Gold Pan Lake at the 7,323 foot level.

Looking down from the road, it appears to be a small mountain lake. Traveling to it by foot from the road is possible, but it is a long, hard and dangerous climb down to the lake. It is an even harder climb back up the mountain side.

There are many miles of horse and hiking trails that start at Kim Creek Camp Ground. Some of the trails lead to Gold Pan Lake and various points in the area near and around Salmon Mountain.

Gold Pan Lake is nestled in a small valley on the slopes of Salmon Mountain. It is a lake where we have seen a cow moose enjoying her evening snack of water lilies and other aquatic plants. Also, it has offered us some excellent trout fishing, followed shortly by a very tasty fried trout dinner served with instant "pistachio pudding" for desert.

This first elk hunt was definitely a "do-it-yourself project." The four of us had zero experience with Elk Hunting. We started out by reading various accounts of what others had done to prepare for their hunts.

<u>The American Hunter</u>, <u>Sports Afield</u> and other outdoor magazines were read and reviewed for tips, suggestions and good advice on what to do and what not to do. I read several books on elk and elk hunting; from them I gained ideas too. If you are interested in an elk hunt, visit your local library. If they do not have the ones you want, they can order them from other libraries. Also, using a public library will save you money.

<u>Elk and Elk Hunting</u> by Hartt Wixom, published by STACKPOLE BOOKS, is a very good over view of elk and elk hunting. It is a good starting point for a beginner.

Before we headed west, we bought elk calls, local maps, topographical maps and an 8'x10' canvas wall tent. We had cots, sleeping bags and an 80,000 BTU propane heater with us. We were fairly well prepared. Our preparation was much better than our first "unprepared" Up North deer hunt in 1952.

We had taken the time to do some of the exercises, walking and running, lifting, pulling; that was needed to be ready for a strenuous hunt in the mountainous terrain. We practiced our elk bugling; our goal was to try and imitate the elk's famous "bugle." We even went to a local elk ranch in southern Minnesota to practice our calling skills.

I soon learned I was poor at calling elk. When Steve Quade called, the ranch elk responded favorably. To us that was encouraging.

Even with our exercising and earlier workouts, we ran into several problems. One of us had to take it easy for a day or two to become acclimated to the thin air in the higher elevation. The physical preparation work we had done in Minnesota was just not enough. It took a couple days of hiking to become comfortable with the ups and downs of the rocky Bitterroot Mountain terrain. Remember, the average "above sea level" elevation in Minnesota is 900'. Depending where you will hunt in Idaho it may be 3,000' to over 10,000' above sea level. You will find that it makes a difference in your breathing.

Once we had set up camp, we had a day and a half to explore the area. We climbed up and down several mountain sides as we were trying to figure out just where to actually hunt.

In our camping area there was another camper who had a moose permit. He, to no avail, had been there moose hunting for almost two weeks. During that time he had seen elk in the area of the camp. He told us they came up from below, and over Lookout Point and meandered right through the camp ground.

Because, my daughter, Terry, could only hunt the first week we had basically two plans for the hunt. That first week the two Steves would pair up, and Terry and I would hunt together. The second week would be left open to what the two Steve's and I felt would be best after the first week.

During the first week we only saw one elk between the four of us. It was at the time Terry and I were following some advice from an article on elk hunting in an <u>American Hunter Magazine</u>. The article had described how bull elk would seek out cooler places to bed down during the day. The highest end of a ravine on the north and west sides of a mountain was mentioned as the kind of place they liked.

Terry and I were hunting on the backside of Dead Top Mountain and walking from one ravine to another. Our plan was to hunt the upper portions of the numerous ravines in the area. As we approached them I would have Terry cover the top of the ravine and I would enter the ravine 75 to 100 yards below her. In this way, we might be able to have a bull elk expose itself somewhere between the two of us. Hopefully, the animal would rise up from a bed and head up hill. One of us, if it worked out that way, would have an opportunity to harvest a bull elk.

Terry would cover the top side of a ravine, and I would enter approximately 100 yards below her. We must have tried that method on 8 to 10 ravines without any luck. That method, of hunting, seemed to be working, we just needed an elk, to validate it.

The one thing we were learning, from the experience, was why the bull elk liked the ravines. The elk could stay cool; in fact, it was very cool, if not cold, in every one of them.

We soon came to another ravine and Terry was to my right, at the head of the ravine. As I indicated above I was about 100 yards to her left as I started walking into the ravine. I soon caught a movement of an elk to my left, I stopped.

The elk moved to the edge of the ravine, our plan was working. The only problem was the elk was to my left, not my right. Before I could do anything, the elk was on his way downhill instead of going uphill.

As he gained speed running down the mountainside, the elk sounded like a freight train. Because Terry was 100 yards to my right, she never saw the elk. I only had a fleeting glance of him. Had I entered the ravine another 50 yards further down the mountain we might've been successful.

The one thing we learned is that the suggestion to "hunt the head of a ravine" was a good one. But, we found out, on a mountain, it takes a lot of walking to go from one ravine to another.

Because we all had licenses for small game and fishing, too, we had several meals of grouse and fish. We would pick up the grouse as we were searching for elk. The three kinds of grouse in the area are ruff, blue and spruce hens. All are excellent eating, especially during a camping trip like this one.

The fish came from Gold Pan Lake. For the most part, we used collapsible spinning rods and reels. The various kinds of casting baits we used were flashy spoons and/or spinner hooks. The fish ranged from ½ to 2 pounds. The fish we ate were always fresh. That's as good as it gets!

The first week ended, and we had only seen one elk between the four of us. Terry had to go back to Pocatello to return to work; the rest of us had to figure out what we were going to do during the second week.

By the end of the first week, we had done a lot of walking throughout the area. Each of us knew our way around the countryside and we were comfortable hunting alone, so we choose that option.

Several more days rolled by and we were not finding the elk. On Tuesday, Steve Sjodin was hunting the area below Lookout Point and he saw one bull elk. Again, it was a fleeting encounter and the animal was gone before he could react.

Wednesday again was another day with no elk sightings. We decided to sleep in Thursday morning. I would make breakfast, we would take a break and then regroup for the last two or three hunting days we had available.

The campsite had an outhouse over by the edge of the drop-off at Lookout Point. I was making breakfast when Quade excused himself to go over and use the outhouse. I told him, "Take your Elk Call and blow the damn thing over the side of the hill!"

He did the call, and soon he was running back to our campsite. He was excited and told us, "I got an answer"! A bull had bugled back.

Wow! He got an answer from a real wild Bull Elk! This was a real surprise to all of us. I was in the middle of fixing breakfast; we had to finish that before we could do anything.

I told the two Steves to go back over to the edge of the steep drop off from the camping area and try calling the elk again. We wanted to see what would happen. They went, came back and said they got another Bull Elk's bugle. Only it was closer this time. Quade said it appeared the elk was moving in our direction. We finished up with breakfast and then we made some plans for a hunt.

We knew the elk herd in the area traveled through the area, about 100 yards right below the outhouse. This was what the other camper told us two weeks earlier. Based on what appeared to be the direction they were moving, we also knew Gold Pan Lake would be the next major area for their movement.

Knowing the direction the herd was moving we decided to have the two Steves position themselves on the hillside below the outhouse. They would try to keep chatter going with the bull elk; in other words "call" him into shooting range.

I, in turn, would go up to the long finger of land overlooking Gold Pan Lake and walk in on it about one-third of a mile. There, I would position myself so I was overlooking a large expanse of territory, territory the elk might cross if they really were heading for Gold Pan Lake.

We put our plan in motion, and I headed for Gold Pan Lake. From my position, I sat there about an hour and then I heard one shot. The sound from the shot came from the wrong direction to be from Quade or Sjodin.

I then heard a bunch of "barking dogs" moving through the pine forest between Lookout Point and Gold Pan Lake. I had never heard a cow elk and how they communicate by "barking" as they "talk" back and forth. The barking, I heard, was the elk herd leaving the area and heading east in a big hurry.

Several hours later, I went down to Gold Pan and started fishing. I caught several trout for supper and returned to camp. Nobody was there to greet me so I started supper. Our favorite meal of fresh trout, mashed potatoes and instant pistachio pudding made with dry milk and water was well under way.

About a 1/2 hour later, they showed up in camp. They were exhausted; I asked them what had happened. They told me the bull they were calling came out of the tree line and started thrashing and tearing apart a small evergreen tree.

They said the bull appeared to be real angry as it was "beating the hell out of a pine tree". Quade, with his 30:06, was right on with his perfectly-placed shot. The result was of his harvesting a very nice 4x5 bull elk.

They said the work started at that point. From the top of the ridge at Lookout Point, to the flatter wooded area below it, where they downed the elk, was a 100-yard steep hillside. The field dressing was done right where the bull elk went down. Sjodin made seven and Quade made six trips up and down that steep hill carrying the meat, hide and antlers of the elk, and their other gear. They were BEAT, TIRED and WORN OUT when they returned to camp.

The shot I heard around 8:30 a.m. in the morning was theirs and it was about 5:30 p.m. when they returned to camp. They had worked over eight hours to successfully finish the work of field dressing, carting the bull up to the truck and then into our camp.

The various articles we had read are very accurate when they say, "The work starts when you put an animal down." The two Steves had just proved it to be a true appraisal of that statement.

Calling that bull elk was a true learning experience; it told us that we could do it. At least Quade could be successful at it. Based on that experience, we decided that the next day, Friday, we would drive to various places along the forest road and try calling. We wanted to see if we could duplicate the return of a bugle call from another bull elk.

Friday morning, we tried calling in several different places with no success. We drove up to Gold Pan Lake, and Quade tried calling from the mountainside overlooking the lake. He gave out a good sounding call and we started to wait. Almost immediately, from the area below and just past the lake, a bull answered. One was below us about a half-mile down another steep mountainside.

I asked the other two if they wanted to pursue the elk that had returned Quade's call. They pondered that question for a few minutes and thought of the potential work ahead. They looked at each other, thought about the steep mountainside, the work involved and said, "NOT TODAY."

They were still beat from the work the day before, and it showed. On Thursday, they had dressed out a good-sized 4x5 bull elk, and between them they had made a dozen trips up and down another steep mountainside and were not ready for another challenge on Friday.

It was too soon for them to try it again! As pointed out many times in the literature, and as we had learned, "The work starts after you down an animal." There was no doubt about that statement being true! In this case one night's rest was just not enough.

The next day was Saturday, and it was time to head home. We packed up our meat and gear and headed for home. We had been hunting for 2-1/2 weeks and had learned a lot about elk hunting. Even though we only saw three elk, we were already starting to think of how soon we could return to the Bitterroots, the Selway River and the Wilderness of Idaho.

After that first hunt, we did return to the Selway Zone four or five times. We were not always as successful. However, on one hunt we had antlerless tags, and we did harvest two antlerless elk. There were six of us in that party.

Twice in the first few years of our new century, we hunted in the Frank Church River of No Return Wilderness Area. We hunted in Area 27 of the Middle Fork Zone. Terry's in-laws, Ray and Millie Leadabrand, owned a cabin at the Middle Fork Ranch. The Ranch is located at the confluence of Pistol Creek and the Middle Fork of the Salmon River. Its 200 acres are located in a large and flat valley which is able to accommodate its own private air strip.

The Frank Church River of No Return Wilderness Area has important Forest Service regulations limiting how you can access the ranch. The four basic ways are by rafting and using the river, by small air craft, by hiking and by horses or mules. Motorized vehicles are prohibited, except by air.

We had different experiences in Area 27 than we did in Area 17. We were using guides, horses and a camp that was already set up. We flew into the ranch. The guides knew the territory, and they knew where the elk usually hung out. They hauled the harvested elk out on horses or mules.

There is no real comparison between the two styles of hunting except that the goal is the harvesting of an elk. In Area 17, we hiked and carried everything on our backs. In Area 27, we had the advantage of horses and the other amenities mentioned earlier.

In 2004, my wife and I moved from St. Peter, MN to Garden Valley, Idaho. Garden Valley is located 50 miles due north of the City of Boise. We lived there for eight years until we moved back to Minnesota in August of 2012.

The home we had was located on a long finger of land on the outlying slopes of Garden Mountain. Our view of Garden Mountain from our living room was picture perfect.

Garden Mountain is about 7,200 feet high, and our home was at the 3,500 foot level. We shared our finger of land with elk, muledeer and whitetail deer. We also had grey wolves, coyotes, mountain lions, red fox, turkeys, grouse and quail sharing it with us.

Living in Area 33 of the Sawtooth Zone offered us another style of elk hunting. In this area we were able to use our off-road vehicles to search for elk and deer sign's and possible places to hunt. Off-road trails are very plentiful in area 33. Terry, Vince, Nicki, Marlene, Paul and I all hunted the area at one time or another for elk and deer using our Polaris Ranger.

In 2006, Marlene, Terry, Nicki (Steve Quade's daughter/my granddaughter) and I had antlerless elk permits for Area 33. In addition to our four elk tags, we all had muzzle loader tags for deer. We filled one with a muledeer buck and the other three with whitetail bucks.

I filled my Muzzle Loader tag with a cow on the last day of the season. The elk was my first of the two cow elk I have harvested.

Marlene and Nicki had been drawn for a special, any weapons, ten-day hunt from December 1-10. On December 1[st,] Marlene filled her tag with a cow elk. Terry filled an elk tag when she was hunting in Area 27, but in area 33 in 2006, she missed an opportunity to harvest an elk with a muzzle loader.

We usually process our own game, and we did all seven animals that December. It took Marlene and me over two weeks to get the job done. The winter was cold and snowy in December, so keeping the meat cold was no problem.

Terry, Nicki, Marlene and I had similar success in 2010. Marlene and I again tackled the big job of processing the one elk and four deer we harvested that year.

The weather and roads from time to time were worse that year. The roads were so bad we could not venture out of our home for several weeks. After that winter, Marlene said she was done doing all the processing. She further said that she was retiring from hunting, and especially from the butchering that is needed.

In our Lean-To-Boys group of hunters, 8 to 10 of us have hunted Idaho for both elk and deer. It all started with that first hunt in the Selway Zone back in the early 1990s. We have used guides in Area 27, done "off-the-road vehicle" hunts in Area 33, and did several do it yourself hunts in Area 17.

Which is the best will depend on what you want out of and/or from a hunt. When I was younger the so called "do it yourself" hunt was a great and welcome challenge. The guided hunts were easier and more productive. The "off the road" hunts meet my physical needs better, especially after hip and knee surgeries. My back injury, a compression fracture in January of 2000, has not helped my hunting.

We had success in all three situations, it's your call. In planning an elk hunt, what you want, what you can physically handle and/or what you can afford will all be major components in any decision you make.

Whatever style of hunt you choose, go for I; you'll never regret it. We have never regretted any elk hunt, and I don't think you will either.

Nicki, as a very happy 14-year old, shown in the photo, filled her elk tag on December 3rd.

Chapter 23

WOMEN AND THE LEAN-TO-BOYS

Charlie Turnbull

I have a son, Vince and three daughters. Vince, in the late 1960s, began his hunting with me on our farm near St. Peter, Minnesota. In 1972, when he turned twelve, he started hunting whitetailed deer. By that time, Junior had three sons hunting with the Lean-To-Boys. When Vince joined our group there was no problem; after all, he was a boy.

My oldest daughter, Charlene, was not interested, at that time, in hunting. My twin daughters, Terry and Mary, indicated they they did have an interest in hunting. If not an interest in hunting, they had a willingness to hunt with their Dad and Brother.

The twin's birthday is early in October. As twelve year olds, they would be eligible to hunt deer in November of 1975. I knew there would be a problem bringing my girls to our male-dominated hunting camp. I needed to coordinate whatever I did with Junior.

I talked to Junior prior to any planning for the fall hunt. There was no doubt that I was taking my girls deer hunting in the fall of 1975. Junior felt our camp of rough-talking males was no place for girls.

Basically, I agreed with him. Although I was not going to bring the girls directly into the Lean-To-Boys camp, we planned to be hunting in the same area. Our camp would be located fairly close to the Lean-To-Boys camp. Even if we were not in their camp, our paths would cross. The exposure for the boys and men of the Lean-To-Boys camp would be a start in their education to the various roles women may take in their lives. Hunting is one such activity.

I ran for Congress in 1972 and in 1974 in Minnesota's Second District. I was keenly aware of the issue of women's rights. Outdoor sports, such as hunting and fishing, need women supporting those activities. The way to have women supporting hunting and fishing is for them to participate in those activities. Participating on an equal level with men is part of the equal rights issue; in my opinion, equality also applies to women who want to hunt.

All three of my daughters were, and are, keenly aware of the issues facing women. They also know the long-range ramifications of them. The bottom line is, "women vote." For all of us to maintain our right to hunt and use firearms responsibly, we need the votes of women as much as those of men.

Now that a decision had been made by my twin daughters, son and I to have our own family party of four, it was time to plan for the trip. The planning that needed to be done was very similar to the planning we did in 1952.

1952 was the first Bigfork, Minnesota deer hunt that Junior and I had planned twenty three years earlier. For that hunt we can say "it was a good prep course." The difference in 1975 was that we were smarter, we had better resources, and we already knew where we were going to be hunting.

Terry and Mary still needed to take and pass a gun safety course. We needed to arrange for Vince and the twins to obtain school excuses for the time they would be out of school.

The kind of shelter we would use was seriously addressed. We also needed to discuss how we would cook the food we planned to take on the deer hunt. Stands and where they were or would be located needed our attention.

Minnesota also required deer hunters to wear red gear. Red gear is the jacket and hat you wear when hunting deer in Minnesota. Later on, the law was changed. We now wear blaze orange for jackets and hats. The State's decision for hunters to use blaze orange clothing has turned out to be a good safety measure.

One area of planning that took very little effort was in determining what firearms we would use for our deer hunt. Vince would use my Remington 300 Savage. Terry would use Marlene's 20 gauge Ithaca shotgun. Mary would use my 20 gauge shotgun and slugs. I had my model 99, 300 Savage.

The gun safety classes that Terry and Mary would take were scheduled late in the summer. They completed the 10 to 12 hours of class and field work and passed the test. That legal hurdle was now behind us.

The question of how to handle and gain the school excuses was handled in a unique way. I took the approach that the premise of schools and education is for teachers to teach and students to learn. Based on that premise, I drafted a note to the grade school for Terry and Mary and one to the high school for Vince. I asked that they be excused to go on an "educational trip," rather than a deer hunting trip, with their father in November of 1975. I told the school that they, as students, would be learning how to track animals, build stands and practice their gun safety skills. In addition, they would learn how to field dress a deer and how to care for the meat. With these experiences and the learning involved, they would be learning an outdoors sport, a sport they could participate in for the rest of their lives. It was my belief that, by putting our hunting trip in terms that educators could relate to, school officials would then excuse the students.

I also knew that it was important to set a good example for my children. Everything in the note was true. If by chance the school would have turned down my request, we would have gone anyway. The difference is that we were being up front and honest. My children were prepared to take the consequences if they were forced to skip school. The important thing is that as a family, we would not be lying and misrepresenting the truth.

The schools did approve of my children's absences. This allowed them to make up any lost work. It was a great learning experience for the whole family.

In 1952, we used a lean-to for our shelter. I suggested to the family that we could do that again. My wife, Marlene, at that point, threw in her two cents worth. She told the four of us to forget it. Marlene knew from our second weekend trip in 1959 just how bad and cold Bigfork weather can be in November. She did not want her daughters to suffer the same fate in 1975 that she did in 1959.

She also said that if we did use a lean-to that I would probably never get the girls to go hunting again. She said that she would buy a slip-in camper for our pickup truck. That was a very pleasant surprise.

With her purchase of a used slip-in camper for our pickup truck, most of our camping problems were solved. The used slip-in camper had beds, a kitchen stove, a refrigerator, a table, a place to store our equipment and a built in heater.

The problems we had in 1952 that related to shelter and sleeping arrangements were taken care of immediately. No sleeping on the ground, we were not going to be cold and we did not have to worry about melting snow or rain getting us wet. If it did happen to rain or snow when we were in the field, we had a place to go, dry off and get warm.

Once we purchased the camper, the questions that remained were relatively minor. We came up with a food list. It was easier to develop because we knew we had the advantage of a propane stove in the camper. Cooking the food would be fairly easy, and the food did not require a lot of advance preparation.

Our clothing and red gear and our stands needed our attention. The four of us had heavy outer clothing. Footwear and red gear needed to be purchased, or borrowed. Vince and I had our hunting gear. The twins however needed red gear and boots.

Good footwear is very important. When your feet get cold, you do not want to sit on a stand. What I used for boots in the 1960s and 1970s were army surplus Korean boots. They were readily available, and I had purchased several pairs over the years. This style of boot served me well for many years. Vince had his own winter boots. The twins used pull-on boots, ones they had for cold and snowy days.

During the late summer and fall, we would go over to our farmland near Norseland, ten miles WNW of St. Peter, Minnesota. On a state map, Norseland is an unincorporated town on MN. Highway 22. There we had opportunities to practice and to develop our marksmanship skills.

It was, and is, important for all of us to practice and become good marksman with our firearms. I felt that my children needed to develop good marksmanship skills.

Gun safety means that you hit the target you are aiming at. If you miss, you will hit something. Let me repeat; the object of gun safety is to make sure your bullet will go where you want it to go. It is as important for hunters to have good marksmanship as it is for Marines, Police and other service men and service women.

With the camper packed, we were ready to head north to Bigfork, Minnesota. The trip to Bigfork would take at least four or five hours. We left Friday morning around 7 a.m. We arrived in Bigfork at 11:30 a.m. That gave us the remaining five hours of daylight to scout the area.

Those five hours also allowed us to make sure that our stands were ready and/or we could build one if we had to. Taking care of the stands would be the last element of preparation that we had to do prior to opening morning.

We were fortunate to have fairly dry and mild weather that year in the Bigfork area. In a lot of ways, it reminded me of the weather we had our first year, in 1952. In a wet year we sometimes had trouble getting through the mud holes. Because of the dryness, we were able to drive all the way to where the logging road crossed the creek.

We found a good spot next to the logging road to park our camper. We faced the truck into the woods. In that way. the back door of the camper faced the road. That made it easy for us to get in and out of the camper. The actual area where we parked was an area that the lumberjacks and lumber companies previously used for their camps and lumber mills many years ago.

The sawdust piles and the slab piles that had been there twenty five years earlier were no longer visible. They had decayed back into the earth. The woods and forest in the camping area had started to mature. Now there were signs of recent logging throughout the area.

The new breed of loggers, with their chainsaws, log skidders and trucks, were harvesting the poplar trees. Forty miles separate Grand Rapids and Bigfork, Minnesota. In Grand Rapids, there is a large paper mill. The poplar and pine trees harvested in the Bigfork area are used by the mill for paper production. A crop of poplar trees can be harvested every 25 to 30 years. They are a great renewable resource.

Our camp's location allowed for easy access to the logging roads that we would be walking on to reach our hunting stands. Mary and Terry had not hunted in the area. Vince had hunted for the last three years at the Lean-To-Boys camp. With Vince leading the way, we left our camp, and headed out to check on our stands,.

We crossed the creek and took the logging road to the left, heading north. Vince's stand was about a half-mile north of the main logging road. When we reached the old stand, the one we had selected for him, we saw we had some work to do. We had to clear some brush along the logging road so that Vince would be able to see 100 yards north and south. We also made sure that he could see up and down the creek and grassy area to the west.

With Vince's stand in place and ready to go, we headed further up the trail. We reached the stand that I had previously used. It was still in good condition, and we checked the shooting lanes to make sure that they were clear. Because this stand was in an area that the deer used as a bedding area, and you could only see 25 to 50 yards in various directions, I picked this stand for Terry. The stand was a perfect set-up for Terry and her 20 gauge shotgun and slugs.

I was not going to use a stand. My plan was to drop Vince and Terry off in the morning as we walked out to our hunting area. I knew the road meandered to the north along the creek. There was a spot where I could find a stump to sit on and cover a small ravine.

It was approaching 3 p.m. We headed back to camp. There was a spot for Mary just south of our camp. When we returned to camp it was after 3 p.m. It gave us an hour or two to make sure that her stand was in good shape. When we checked it out, everything looked good. With our work completed we could relax and sit around the camper that evening.

Saturday, the opening day of the 1975 deer season, was here. There was a chill, in the air but it was not cold. It was a great day for the twin's first deer hunt. We had a good breakfast of hamburger, eggs, pancakes and milk. We started out for our stands at 6:30 a.m.

We could shoot starting at 7 a.m. if we were fortunate enough to see any animals. Usually, on the first three mornings, there is a lot of shooting. You hear the shooting coming from all directions.

This year, there were a few shots off in the distance. The shooting was down considerably when compared with other years.

During the mid-1970s, the deer herd in Minnesota was down. The success ratio was low during that time. Although we did some very good planning, it appeared that the deer did not get the message.

I did have a coyote working the drainage gully where I was sitting. With a good shot, I harvested him. Otherwise, the two days of hunting that we had planned turned out to be several nice days in the woods. You might say we got skunked.

The first-year deer hunting trip for the twins was a good start. Even though we did not harvest a deer, it was still a success. We had built two stands, we had fun camping, and the girls had the opportunity to participate in a lifelong form of recreation.

Maybe having a first-time hunt that is not too successful is okay. Just think; if Vince or one of the twins had been successful and by chance had taken a large buck, they might have to go through life never being able to duplicate their first years' experience.

For myself, I was very pleased to be hunting with my son and two of my daughters. We were not in the Lean-To-Boys cabin sharing stories. However, we were sharing the same excitement of a hunt as they did. In our co-ed hunting camp, we were developing our own stories based on new experiences for the girls.

On opening day, as I said, I did see and shoot a brush wolf. They are commonly called coyotes. Bears, wolves and coyotes are great animals. Many hunters are not overly elated with them. They compete with men for the available wildlife, and, in some cases, aid in the depletion of the herd and/or number of small animals.

Most hunters are aware that bears are the biggest problem in the spring. They feed on deer fawns and elk and moose calves.

Wolves also take the fawns and calves. Wolves, because of their hunting skills, can and will take down and kill the largest elk or moose available.

The biggest problem bears present is in the spring. Bears have not eaten all winter. In the spring, they come out of hibernation hungry. The deer, elk and moose have just dropped their fawns and calves, providing a good meal for a hungry bear.

For the first month or two the calves and fawns are very vulnerable, making them easy prey for the bears. There are many people who feel that black bears (grizzlies out west) are a bigger problem than wolves for elk, deer and moose.

The first time that the twins and Vince hunted together was in 1975. It was a start, and the twins continued hunting with Vince and me as a family unit from 1976 to 1978. The four years we hunted as a family were not overly productive. We did harvest one deer in each of the three years after 1975.

Vince's stand overlooked a beaver pond. He could watch up and down the creek and cover both sides of it. It was a good area, one where the deer crossed the creek. His stand was only three feet off the ground.

It had rails around its sides to lean on and a bucket to sit on. Today, we would say it was a bit primitive.

In 1975, the weather was mild and sunny. The second year, 1976, was cold, the beaver pond in front of his stand was frozen over. We also had 8 to 10 inches of snow on the ground. The pond's ice was more than 6 inches thick and very safe to walk on. Even though it was cold, it was not unbearable.

The good part in dealing with the weather was our having the "slip-in" camper. In the camper, we had a propane heater and a way to stay warm. As the only adult in camp, it was one less thing for me to worry about. The camper made hunting with my kids an enjoyable outing.

Mary had her stand just south of our campsite. She and Vince were close enough together so that they could help each other out or share any work that needed to be done. She had heard Vince's shot and walked over to his stand. I was hunting north of Vince and had heard the shot also. I waited for a half hour and then started working my way back to Vince. Mary was there and greeted me when I showed up.

Mary said to follow me, which I did. She walked across the beaver pond to its far side. She pointed down to the snow and said, "Do you see those tracks?" Obviously, I could see them. "Yes, I can see them." Again, she told me to follow her. We walked about 25 yards, and she pointed at Vince's six point buck lying on the edge of the pond.

She was more excited about his success than he was. She was so animated I could hardly believe it. She was so pleased and happy for Vince and his first deer. You would have thought that she was the one who harvested her first buck.

Now the work and training fell onto my shoulders. A lesson for two of my kids was in order. This was the first time I was able to field dress a deer with their help.

The field dressing of the deer went well. We completed the job in a reasonable amount of time. It, also, was the first time they had an opportunity to drag a deer to camp.

We hunted the rest of the day and the next day, too. Our hunting for the rest of the weekend had been to no avail. We were very happy to leave Bigfork with Vince's nice buck.

In 1977, we used the same stands as the previous two years. That year, there were 17 combined hunters in the two camps, the Lean-To-Boys camp and the Turnbull's Family camp.

The deer herd was way down, and Minnesota was now using a buck law. Only antlered deer could be taken. In order to be legal, the antlers had to be at least 3 inches in length. In many ways, it was a poor year for young hunters.

From my experience, "It is important for young hunters to have some initial successes." The mid and late 1970s was not a good time to help young hunters build their enthusiasm for deer hunting.

This was one of those down years for deer hunting. The Lean-To-Boys did not harvest a deer on opening day. For 13 hunters in their camp, that was basically unheard of. None of us would have predicted that.

A surprising thing for us happened that day. Terry not only saw a deer, she was able to harvest a fork horn buck. The buck came to her stand from her back side. She heard it rustling the dry leaves. When she turned to look, she was SURPRISED, to see a fork horn buck! She was successful in turning just enough to get a good and accurate shot. Her practice time on our rifle range paid off!

Again, I had the privilege of training another one of my children in the art of field dressing a deer. After we completed field dressing the deer, we headed back to camp. Again, just like the year before, we continued hunting over the weekend. Again, as a family we headed for home, pleased with Terry's success and with venison for our freezer.

In 1978, we did things very differently than in the previous years. The DNR came up with a different style of deer hunting. Instead of a nine day season they opened the whole month of November for deer hunting.

Although, that may sound good, it wasn't. The whole month of November was available. The catch was how many days each hunter could hunt. Prior to this change, a hunter could hunt all nine days of the season. The new system had two basic options. The options were three days or five days. If you chose the three-day option, you hunted the first week-end in November. If you waited to go hunting after the first few days of the month, you could select any consecutive five-days for your hunt. The five days we chose were over the four-day Thanksgiving weekend.

Because our family chose the Thanksgiving weekend, we had the original Lean-To-Boys cabin all to ourselves. By hunting over the four-day Thanksgiving weekend, we did not need to seek permission from their schools to take the time off.

On the Wednesday before Thanksgiving, we left Faribault, heading for Bigfork. It was a late start. By the time school was out, we were totally loaded, and had supper it was close to 7 p.m. We used the camper/pickup for our travel to and from Bigfork.

It was after midnight when we finally reached the logging road, the one that would lead us to the Lean-To-Boys cabin. Because of the snow, we had to leave our truck on the "minimum-maintenance road."

The cabin was over a mile down the logging road. It was a long cold walk in below-zero weather. With our gear and equipment piled on a toboggan and our food in our packs, we headed east to the cabin.

I knew our midnight journey would be a cold walk. At the cabin, we would be able to start a fire in the woodstove. We would be fine once we made it to the cabin.

The cabin was as cold inside as the air on the outside. That cabin's coldness was a motivator for our starting a fire in the woodstove.

With the fire finally roaring, it still took several hours for the cabin to warm up. It finally did get warm; not hot, but warm enough if you were wearing a sweater.

Once the cabin was warm we had the same comforts as we had in the camper. It certainly offered us warmth, a place to cook, and good bunks. What more could you want on a subzero night?

It was early morning before we had a chance to get some sleep. After a half hour of tossing and turning, I was finally able to sleep. Sleep only lasted about three hours.

When I woke up, it was daylight and somewhere around 8 a.m., we were not off to an early start. We fixed a light breakfast and headed for our stands. The stands we used in other years were not used this time. We used stands that were closer to the cabin.

After I knew the twins and Vince were on their stands, I headed to the well stand. Along the way, I was watching for deer tracks, but I did not cross any along the way. I passed by the well stand and continued on to the fender stand.

At the fender stand, I chose to walk east on the survey line. I walked approximately a half mile to a spot where, all of a sudden the woods opened up. The open area had recently been logged off, and I was able to overlook the 80 acres of cleared terrain.

This was the first major cutting I had seen in the areas we hunted. It was something I did not expect. I just stood there and looked over the terrain. I again started to make my way further east. I had the poplar forest on my right and the open area to my left.

Shortly, I spotted a doe about 300 yards to the northeast of me in the logged over area to my left. I was hunting with my Model 99, 300 Savage and shooting offhand. I took the shot and the doe immediately crumpled into a pile right where she was standing. As I walked to where the deer had fallen, I counted 280 paces.

I took the time to field dress the doe. I then headed for our cabin. My children were there warming up and having lunch. I showed them the heart of my doe, and told them I needed their help in dragging the deer to camp.

By now, everybody was warm and ready to go. The approximately one and a half mile drag of the deer back to the cabin would require a team effort. We headed out to where I left the deer. Dragging the deer back to camp took several hours.

It was not hard work, and the ten inches of snow helped in sliding the deer over the terrain. With four of us, we could trade off on the pulling. None of us were ever over worked.

In the four years we hunted, as a family, at Bigfork, we only harvested three deer. Two of my four children harvested their first deer. As luck would have it, they both were bucks. It was a good start for all of them.

Terry and Mary were wrapped up in high school events. By the time they were freshmen in high school they were active in several sports. Both were very good swimmers, and swimming is a fall sport. They also participated in drama and other school activities. For the next four years, these activities became their priority. Hunting took a back seat.

In the four years we hunted the Bigfork area, we had one serious situation we had to handle. Bigfork is known for its waterholes on the logging roads we use. One situation was serious because the pickup with the camper got stuck halfway through one swampy area. Earlier we had driven through it and parked by the creek. Everything had gone very well on the way into our camping area. On the way out I must have taken the wrong set of ruts through the long waterhole. Soon, we were stuck.

We were basically prepared for almost any situation. We were even prepared with equipment to aid us if we did get stuck. We had several tow chains, heavy rope, a "come-a-long winch" and a chainsaw. We soon found out that we did not have enough chain or rope for us to use the come-a-long winch. We were approximately 25 feet short. Mary said, "Dad what do we do now?" I told her not to worry, and that I have an idea, for making an extension for the chains. "Right Dad" was the first thing I heard from Mary. All I could tell her, and the other two was to watch.

I asked Vince to cut down two five to six-inch poplar trees. We trimmed off all the branches and cut them into 18-foot poles. I asked him to cut a saw mark almost half way through (18 inches up from the butt end of each pole.) Next, he measured another 20 inches up the pole and made an identical cut.

Vince then cut out the wood between the cuts. He now had two notches, one on each 18' pole. At that point, I turned one pole around and placed the two butt end notches together like Lincoln Logs. We used a rope to tie them together. Now we had an extension for our chains.

It was approximately 30 feet long. We could now hook one end of a chain to a tree. The other end of the chain was tied to our make-shift extension. On the other end, we did the same thing by using the come-a-long winch. The difference was it was hooked up between the pickup and the make-shift extension.

So now we had a stuck pickup truck with a slip-in camper hooked up to a come-a-long wibch, hooked up to a chain that was hooked up to the poplar tree extension. The extension, in turn, was two poles with notches and tied together in the extensions middle. The extension was tied to a tree, which served as the anchor on the other end from the stuck truck. Nothing to it, I thought.

The whole thing was working, and we had made approximately 10 feet of progress. Then, we had a little luck. The Lean-To-Boys had just broke camp and were leaving.

There was some grumbling, but they pitched in and helped by pushing us out of the waterhole. I'm sure that their help saved us anywhere from 2 to 4 hours of hard work with the come-a-long winch and our make-shift extension.

Since those days in the mid-1970s, several other of the Lean-To-Boys have had their wives, significant others, or girls involved in deer hunting. Not at the Lean-To-Boys cabin or camp, but in areas and camps located adjacent to or close by in the area east of Bigfork.

They did it like our family had to do it; they set up camps in adjacent areas. Now they join us for supper at our Friday evening steak fry. All in all, I think it has shown a level of acceptance not there years ago.

Because my girls held their own and demonstrated that they, too, could hunt, they became recognized as hunters. Seven or eight years later, Terry, during the bear season, harvested a black bear out of the Lean-To-Boys camp. They, along with their mother, deserve some credit in expanding women's role and acceptance in the hunting and shooting sports.

As a parent, rewards show up every now and then. One day, my daughter, Mary told me that her husband had asked her how she ever learned to do so many things. She told him that she had hunted and worked with her father and knew how to make things work.

She recounted her experience making the extension of a chain from poplar trees. She told Kip "Every once in a while, we had to improvise to make things work on the farm or when we were hunting." I always felt her comments were a great compliment to our hunting and working together years ago as a family.

Her twin sister, Terry, still hunts, but she puts more time on raft trips. She was once referred to as the "river woman" because of her skill, love and interest in rafting and kayaking in the whitewater rivers of the northwest.

My oldest daughter, Char, took up hunting later and hunted for approximately 20 years. Her deer hunting in Minnesota was all at our farm in St. Peter, Minnesota. There, she used a 12 gauge and slugs and became very skilled with it. She now lives in Idaho, and has dropped hunting in favor of her law practice.

Mary hunted several years at the farm, on the second weekend hunts. The last year she hunted she was successful in filling her deer tag. She set up the St. Peter High School Girls' Swimming Program and gave up hunting in favor of coaching the swim team.

Vincent and I still hunt every season with the Lean-To-Boys. Once in a while, I can get my wife or one of the girls to hunt with me the second weekend on our land near St. Peter, Minnesota.

I have one granddaughter in Idaho who hunts elk and deer with me. I have another one in Minnesota, who someday again might hunt; with her mother as her coach, high school swimming always took precedence in the fall.

One thing I know, as a person who has encouraged women to hunt, I can tell you that they are as much fun at a camp as a camp full of men ever were. Deer hunting is a great sport for both sexes.

As time goes on, deer hunting may be the only hunting available for both women and men. As we lose land, waterholes and habitat that once were available for pheasant and duck hunting, it appears deer and now turkeys, are the only wild game gaining and holding their own.

If you never had an opportunity to take or go with your family hunting or fishing, it is time to do so. You'll never regret it. I haven't.

Chapter 24

'NEW IN CAMP'

Steve Quade was new to the Lean-To-Boys hunting camp in the early 1990s. Not as a new hunter, but as an experienced one. He had been deer hunting successfully for years with his family near their home northwest of Garrison. He also had done some serious duck hunting with my son and me on our farm near St. Peter.

He had a real advantage because he knew most of the hunters in our camp. Still, you have to fit in when you join a hunting party. His chapter "New in Camp" touches on being new, and how you learn the ins and outs of how to fit into a hunting camp.

Chapter 24
New in Camp
Steve Quade

The Lean-To-Boys Camp is always open to those of us who want to show up and talk about past hunts, recent hunts, future hunts, the problems of life and just about anything else. The atmosphere is friendly and you are sharing experiences with people who care about the same things you do.

Over the years the camp has moved from a lean-to for shelter to a legitimate cabin. A cabin, for our shelter has worked out the best. The weather has had a lot to do with the types of shelters the Lean-To-Boys have relied upon and developed over the years.

Weather can be extreme with excessive rain in the spring and fall. Deep snow is characteristic of winter weather. Summers can be very hot and humid.

The winters can be very cold. Thirty to forty below zero are expected for extended spells most winters. On the other hand we can have beautiful Indian summers that extend late into the month of November.

I started hunting with the group in the early 1990s. Since that time many things have changed. I have lived through the first cabin, the squad tent and now the second cabin. The number of hunters has gone from 6 to 8 and now up to 14 or 15. The people and the stories they tell also have changed. At this time we have three generations of hunters in the camp. I am in the middle.

Work weekends are part of the experience at our camp. They give us a chance to gather wood, clean up the cabin, add another mouse trap to the trap line and enjoy another weekend in the woods of northern Minnesota. The work weekends also give each of us a chance to check out our stands.

As I mentioned the spring and fall rains are often plentiful. The rain aids the growth of vegetation around our stands. Our shooting lanes need to be cleared of brush. If we do not clear the shooting lanes we can miss opportunities of seeing and harvesting a deer.

Most of the work weekend activities are discussed and decided on the first evening when we arrive at camp. In the morning the planning is reaffirmed before we head out to our stands. One thing I know is that it appears chaotic the first time or two you go through a work weekend.

After a couple of these weekends you start to see a thread of organization. The form of the organization is central to accomplishing whatever needs to be done.

I found out in the beginning you had to watch the old Marines and the way they operate. They were used to organizing the troops and getting things accomplished.

At first I did a lot of listening and watching. As time went on I found you could suggest alternatives to such things as deer stand designs or modification of them, menus and things that needed to be done or changed.

The camp composition has changed over the years. Hunters may be added based on recommendations made by those of us who are currently involved in the camp. The recommendations for newcomers to our hunting camp are prescreened in an informal way.

Bringing in a new hunter also means taking a look at the stands we are using and who will be using them. Once in a while if the hunter is new, for example a twelve year-old, we usually have the father supervising the young hunter.

The stands that we use eventually end up with a name. For example there is Charlie's stand. It used to be Terry's stand. You might hear one or the other of those two names for the same stand. For the most part however each stand has only one name. We have the well stand, Mike's stand, Chuck's stand, the survey line, the fender stand, the creek stand, the wolf stand and several others.

Each stand has its own history and stories to tell. Obviously the stand does not tell the stories about the deer harvested, missed opportunities or the other animals that frequent the area. It is the hunters who use the stand who weave the tales.

The stories and tales told by the hunters have given each stand its own character, history and uniqueness. When someone says Junior shot a buck at the 'well' everybody knows exactly where he shot his buck. In a sense the stands are an integral part of each hunter's experience at our camp.

The Lean-To-Boys Camp is more than a handful of guys getting together to go hunting. It is about people who together have shared many life experiences. In a sense there is comfort in getting together and everyone knowing we made it through another year and we are looking forward to the next year.

At this deer camp, age and experience are important and looked up to. The people who have the experience share it with the new hunters. Once you are a member of the Lean-To-Boys Camp you are a partner and equal sharing a place at the table with everybody.

The actual hunting has been one of the great pleasures of my life. Various stands are usually available. One year many of the stands that are way out and away from our camp were not producing any game. Several of us started hunting in stands closer to the cabin.

I climbed into one of those stands and took a good look around the area. Several hours later I had a deer moving quickly across the trail. I kept watching the deer and was waiting for an opening in the woods. I finally had my opportunity to shoot.

After I shot I waited for 10 to 15 minutes before climbing down from the stand. I walked over to where the deer had dropped and to my surprise I had a nice eight pointer. The change in stands I made that day worked out well for me.

For several years I was using the wolf stand. Each year I had to clear the brush and grass that had grown up in my shooting lanes. Each year I would push the brush back a little bit further than the year before. As time went on the stand was improving.

Although I had been using the wolf stand for several years I got bumped out of the stand. It belonged to Chuck. He was the one who established the stand.

Chuck's son, who had just turned twelve, was going to start hunting with us. He needed a good stand, one where he wouldn't get lost and one close enough to his dad for supervision. This forced me to go out and search several other areas.

There was an area approximately three and a half miles southeast of our camp they told me could be a good area. Bob used to hunt there years ago. I checked it out and found the lanes and stand needed some, really a lot of, attention.

The area, however, looked promising. I removed dead falls, brush and grass in the shooting lanes. I rebuilt the stand, at 220 pounds I wanted to make sure it would stand up under my weight.

Over the years the stand has been very productive for me. There's one board built into the stand where I cut notches every time I'm successful in harvesting a deer.

One of my memories that I will take to my grave was the opening day 2007. On that day I was sitting in my stand fairly well relaxed when there was a rustling of some leaves or brush.

I looked in the direction of the noise and there were five Timberwolves only 30 feet away. I must have been well concealed in my stand to have those five wolves come within 30 feet of me.

In the many years we have hunted the area there have only been seven or eight wolf sightings. The other sightings were of one or two wolves. Seeing five at one time was real unique and probably a once in a lifetime experience.

That day I did not see any deer. I have to assume the deer moved out of the area. Another part of the same story happened the next day. From what I could see, there were no wolves, in the area. I did have a nice buck show up and I harvested him. I had the pleasure that year of adding another notch in my stands trophy board and a wonderful memory of five wolves.

Many times I have sat in my stand as the sun pierces and darts through the morning cold. The sunlight not only brings light to the woods it also warms me. The beams of light make the water droplets from the heavy dew to sparkle in the grass. It is another one of those enjoyable times as you sit and bring in a new day.

Sometimes people think all you do is hunt animals. We do that but there is much more to it than just harvesting an animal. Sitting on the stand and being quiet allows me the chance to become part of the total environment.

On a daily basis I have chickadees land on the tree limbs only inches away from my face and hands. They are a friendly bird, it is fun to watch them flitter from branch to branch pecking away at the bark looking for a breakfast.

During the day I have the pleasure of watching a ruff grouse working its way under my stand and scratching for food. Other times when there was snow they would sit on a birch bark tree branch and feast on the trees seed cones.

If the crows find an owl you could bet that you are going to hear them pestering the owl all day long. In the evening I would see them flying in groups of 10 to 20 heading for their roosting area. For me all of these little interruptions are part of what makes me enjoy sitting on a stand. I can sit all day and enjoy it even if I don't see any deer.

In the morning after I get settled and make sure everything is in place I can then break out a book and enjoy reading it. It is important to be alert but you can read a book, be quiet, take time to look around and then repeat the sequence over and over all day. As I said the birds and other animals also breakup portions of your day.

As I'm sitting there and I'm checking and looking over the terrain I catch a shadow moving through the brush. It has my attention. The shadow takes the familiar form of a deer. I can tell where he's headed because other deer have used the same trail. I raise my gun and focus my eyes on the image as the deer appears in my scope. Even though I've done this many times my heart still starts beating and pounding. It seems as if I'll always have that pounding and surge of adrenaline when I first see the deer. I hope I never lose it.

I now have the deer fully exposed in my scope and he has moved into the position I was counting on for my shot. I took the shot and harvested another buck. I have to field dress my deer, but before I do I'm going to add another notch to the stand.

Shortly the commotion caused by my shot, the cutting of the notch, and field dressing of the deer have subsided. I am now again sitting, reading, waiting and enjoying the birds and other animals that have been given to me by Mother Nature. I might see another deer today. It really doesn't matter I have had another wonderful day by myself in the woods I have come to love.

At camp that night I had several new stories to tell. At camp, as I was telling my stories, I found, I also had a great group of hunters ready to listen to them. Being 'new in camp' was a few years ago; I've found I can tell and share stories just as good as everybody. I think the newness is wearing off.

Chapter 25

DEER CAMP FARE

My son Vince, loves food. He has worked in the food field most of his life as a cook, a restaurant manager and as a pizza company employee. He has worked in several other lines of work, too; R.V. sales, Home Depot, and a landscaping business are the most notable.

Recently, he started working on food production as a producer of grapes and garden vegetables. He, Kathy Gullaiye and his friend, Joe Miller purchased a home on five to six acres just outside of Vernon Center, Minnesota. They are getting into the field of sustainable farming.

Taking on the job of camp cook was a natural for Vince. Our former cook, Jim Smith, had the job for 30 to 40 years. Jim joined our camp when he dissolved the Smith hunting party. Jim had been a cook in the army. When he joined our party, we all felt he was a natural for the job of camp cook. Although Vince wasn't a cook when he was in the service, he has had lots of experience cooking in commercial restaurants.

There are always some problems when the hunting camp changes cooks. Some of the recipes are changed by the new cook. The most notable change with Vince was the "SOS" recipe. The reason nobody complains too much is because they're afraid the cook will hand them the spatula and let them do the cooking.

Chapter 25
Deer Camp Fare
Vince Turnbull

I am the new Lean-To-Boys Camp cook. During the first weekend of each deer season it is a two or three day part time job. The pay is only the praise or complaints I get after a meal.

I am a third generation hunter in the camp. One thing we know and have found out over the years is that every once in a while we need a new cook. I guess I volunteered for the job.

There might have been a little 'leaning' on me from Junior to get me to be a volunteer. Jim was pushing 75; Junior knew Jim needed to retire as the 'camp cook'. Anyway I like cooking and it's has worked out very well. My taking over the menu and cooking was an obvious progression.

The Lean-to-Boys have progressed from being "The tough guys" sleeping under pine trees and stands consisting of all the comforts of a stump. With the younger 'Boys' and their sons now in camp and our capabilities in making better and tastier meals there are and have been changes.

I have been told that in the good old days they only did just enough cooking to get by. A few hot dishes were brought from home and used for the evening meals. We still use the hot dishes but we have added much more.

Of course breakfast is the number one meal on the first day of the deer hunting season. As the Camp Cook making sure that first day's breakfast is a number one experience is the most important part of the job.

Over the years we have had several other hunters serve as the 'camp cook'. At first my dad, Charlie did some of the cooking. He was followed by another member of the party, Bob, who cooked for a year or two. I only started hunting in 1972 so I do not know how good any of the early cooks were.

Jim followed Bob and he was the cook when I started hunting. He did the cooking for several decades.

Years ago they only had 3 to 6 hunters in camp. Now we have 12 to 15 hunters in camp; 2012 was huge with 18 in camp (I am sure it is my cooking). I have had experience cooking in several restaurants including the big V.F.W. Club in Fargo, North Dakota and as a Chef at the 'Stump Supper Club' out on Roberds Lake in Rice County. Compared to that, cooking for 12 to 15 hunter's has not been too difficult.

Breakfast as I said before is the main meal. It gets us started in the morning on opening day. SOS has become our number one breakfast.

Everyone likes SOS, because it tastes good, it is simple and has been a tradition for decades. What has made this the Opening Day staple is they can have all they want, it is a 'stick to your ribs' fare that carries you through the morning and wards off any midmorning hunger pains.

I feed from 12 to 15 people on the first two days of the season. The big pot of SOS I make is enough for both mornings. Another part of this, if needed, is the fact that it can be stretched with whole milk and some spices for the second day.

S.O.S is short for 'Stuff on a Shingle' (the 'Politically Correct' version of the name). The Stuff part is similar to Sausage Gravy and the Shingle is the toast. I start this whole process at about 4 o'clock on opening morning. We have found English muffin bread really works well for the "shingle" part of SOS. It toasts up easily and offers us the best flavor.

The SOS is the mainstay of the breakfast meal. We always have coffee, juice, milk, toast and peanut butter and jelly available too. Nobody leaves for their stand hungry because of a lack of food for breakfast. If they do, it's their own damn fault.

For your information I am including two recipes for our SOS. The recipes, it must be noted are for various numbers of hunters. They can be modified up or down depending on the number of hunters in your camp. Of course you'll have to use a little math to accomplish any recipe modification.

Both recipes are very good, I just prefer mine to Jim's. There was a little "grousing" the first time I changed the SOS recipe. It died down fairly quickly. I guess nobody really wanted to take over the spoon I use for stirring and serving the SOS.

The first recipe is the one Jim used. It was the way he did it as a cook in the army and then at our hunting camp. The second is the one I use.

Jim's Lean-To Boys SOS Recipe

2 lbs. of ground venison or beef browned and/or pork sausage
1/2 gallon of "canned" Milk
1-½ cups Wondra flour
Salt and Pepper to taste
2 loaves of bread {for the shingles)

Take the browned meat and put it in a large pot, add the canned milk and flour and heat over med to high heat stirring until thickened.

Ladle over the shingles, serve and enjoy. Feeds [+or-] 8-10

Vince's Lean-To-Boys SOS Recipe

1 lb. ground venison or beef browned
2lbs. Jimmy Dean pork sausage browned
1 teaspoon garlic powder
2 tablespoons sugar
1 gallon 2% milk
1 tablespoon fresh ground black pepper
3 cups flour
3 tablespoons dehydrated chopped onions
4 loaves English muffin toasting bread. Toast the bread (i.e., make the shingles) in an 8 qt. pot add milk, flour, garlic powder, pepper and sugar. Heat the mixture over medium to high heat stirring until thickened. Add the browned meat and stir for several more minutes.

Ladle over the shingles, serve and enjoy. Feeds 12-14

In the morning we get up at 4 AM and I start preparing breakfast. Usually breakfast is ready around 5 to 5:30 AM. To be ready in an hour to an hour and a half I need to do a lot of prep work prior to opening day. Some is done at home the rest is done at camp on Friday.

The SOS is a tradition for breakfast, a second tradition are the hot dishes we bring each year. The hot dishes are used for evening meals especially on Saturday, Sunday and the first Monday.

They are prepared in our homes, packed in half gallon milk cartons and frozen. By freezing the hot dishes in the milk cartons we accomplish two things, first they do not perish, second when we pack our food supplies they help to keep the other food cool.

One thing about hot dishes is the convenience they offer along with the variety they offer us in our meals. Most of the time it takes two hot dishes to feed our hunters. The key to using the hot dishes is to make sure we thaw them out. If they are thawed out it only takes 30 to 40 minutes to prepare supper.

When you think about it hot dishes come in countless varieties. Over the years we have identified several hot dishes that are the favorites of the hunters.

A Sauerkraut and Cheese Hot Dish is a favorite that Mike brings. Charlie brings a dish of Potatoes, Hamburger, Carrots and Peas. Scalloped Potatoes and Ham have been on the menu, so has Baked Beans. Punky has brought Mexican and Italian dishes at different times. They all go over well with our hungry hunters.

Lunches are a part of the camps fare too. We always have two or three kinds of luncheon meat on hand for sandwiches. We also offer peanut butter and jelly. Most of the hunters like luncheon meat, a slice of onion and mustard in their sandwiches.

Each hunter adds the condiments such as mayo, ketchup and mustard that they prefer on their sandwiches. One person, usually Charlie, assembles them on Friday evening for each hunter. If we didn't do it that way it would be a disaster trying to have 12 to 15 people all making sandwiches at the same time.

What each hunter wants to drink or munch on is up to them. Once in a while people will come in for lunch at the cabin. Most of the hunters stay out all day and come back to camp after dark.

In the last several decades we have been having a steak BBQ on Friday evening. Several friends and hunters from other nearby camps join us for this event. As the cook I don't have anything to do with the steaks and how they are cooked.

The local Bigfork grocery store Kocions, prior to and during the deer season always has a heavy demand at their meat counter. Most of the demand is for steak. This is especially true on the

Friday prior to the opener. It's best to get there early for the best selection.

If somebody wants to burn their steak to a crisp or eat their meat raw that's their business. I do however pre-bake 25 potatoes. I also put a salad together, a fairly simple one. Lettuce, onions, tomatoes and cucumber slices is enough. I set out two kinds of salad dressing and everybody is happy. If they're not happy they can apply for the job of cook.

Over the years the Friday night steak fry has become a real social event. All of the friends we have made with other hunters and residents of the Bigfork Area are invited. We get a chance to catch up on what's happening in the other camps and in and around the Bigfork area.

This is an event where several women hunters show up. They are some of the wives of the hunters from the nearby deer hunting camps. They too like to participate in the meal, have a beer and join in the lively conversation.

One thing about the Friday night steak fry is the fact, we do not skimp on the meat we eat. Beautiful T-bone, porter house, rib eye, strip steaks and thick pork chops are the main choices for everybody.

To pay our camps expenses, at this time, each hunter in our camp throws $50 in the camp 'kitty'. Food costs run approximately $35 to $40 per person. The other 10 to $15 pays for LP gas and other incidentals. Years ago they got by on $10, but that was 50 to 60 years ago. With the kitty only costing each hunter $50 it turns out to be a pretty good bargain.

It has been that way for about three years. Each hunter can stay two to sixteen days. About half of the hunters on the first weekend arrive on Thursday or Friday and leave on Sunday afternoon. A couple more stay and leave on Monday or Tuesday. The rest might be there for a week or two. Any way you look at it $50 is very reasonable for each hunter.

I am looking forward to my cooking tenure and hunting with the Lean-To-Boys. Who knows I might even come up with a few more changes in the camp menu! I am thinking my basil/tomato soup would be good. It would sit on the woodstove and stay hot for the hunters as they came back to camp for lunch.

'Tradition' is important in our camp. I plan to change some more of the camps menu. The one thing I wouldn't change is SOS on opening morning. You don't mess with tradition, but I might 'tinker' with the menu. After all, new ideas can soon become a tradition too.

In the early 1990s the Lean-To-Boys lost their first cabin. The county owned the land and they put it up for a timber bid. They informed us we had to move our first cabin or they would burn it down. The Lean-To-Boys organized a winter work party to move the equipment and vacate the cabin.

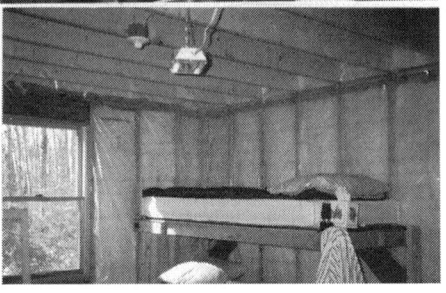

We went back to tenting and we used a squad tent for shelter. The squad tent worked; but it was a poor substitute for our first cabin. The squad tent was always cold. The cook had less than adequate facilities for preparing meals and he had trouble serving warm food. The cold also made our sleeping less than comfortable.

After a couple years I knew we needed to do something different. I asked my dad if I could build a cabin on our 20 acres at Bigfork. Dad gave me the go ahead so I built a new cabin in 1999. At the time I built it I was working for Home Depot. Using a computer at work I was able to design it. I was also able to buy my materials from Home Depot. By using my employee discount privileges I was able to afford the cost of the project.

The cabin I built is much larger than our first cabin. The cabin we now use has one big room for cooking, dining and use as a living room. On the west wall we have a sink, a little counter space and the kitchen stove. The stove is propane fired and has four burners and two ovens.

One of the ovens requires electricity to make it work. For the most part the stove works and we get by.

A woodstove heats the new cabin. It has a large flat area on top. We can heat water on it or use it to keep our food warm prior to it being served. The woodstove works out well for our camp. Without it, having warm food and hot water would not be very feasible.

The wood stove requires good wood; wood that is dried out, aged and ready for our use in November. To keep us warm work parties for cutting and splitting the wood are formed. In that way we get the job done and have the wood we need.

Pictured is the new cabin as it was being built, the kitchen area and one of the cabin's two bedrooms.

The new cabin's kitchen is more spacious than any we had in the past. Even so there is a table in the kitchen that is used by the cook.

That table is a must; it adds the needed counter space I need when preparing meals and feeding everybody.

Some of the work that needs to be done are the projects that were never finished; eventually, however we'll get to them. In the meantime we enjoy the comforts of a good cabin. A cabin on our own land with no fear of losing it; we did that once and prefer not to have a repeat of it.

We do not have running water. We have to carry in the water. The electricity we have is provided by a generator. Our toilet facilities are outside the cabin, in what is commonly called an "out house." The bottom line is we're inside, warm, well fed and managing very well.

For the land purchase we have to thank the two oldest Lean-To-Boys in our camp. In the mid-1990s, Junior and my dad, Charlie, purchased the original 80 acres. Later the 80 acres was sub-divided into four twenty acre parcels. Because of their land purchase and the new cabin everybody has enjoyed better living quarters.

As the camp cook I know my kitchen is easier to work in than the more crowded ones we had before. I am looking forward to a long tenure as the Lean-To-Boys cook. That is, providing nobody decides to take the job of cook over; all they have to do is complain too much and they will be handed the spatula and cooks apron.

Chapter 26

A TRUE BIRD HUNTER

Junior's fourth son, Steve, has become an avid bird hunter. He loves hunting ducks, turkeys, pheasants and quail. Of course, he doesn't do it in Minnesota. He lives and works in Minnesota. He hunts ducks in North Dakota, and upland game, including turkeys, in Kansas.

So that he would have a place to hunt upland game in Kansas, he went so far as to purchase a quarter section of land in that state. He travels to Kansas several times a year, just to hunt quail, turkeys and pheasants.

Over a period of time, he has added the needed habitat to his land, which in turn aids in building the quail, turkey and pheasant populations. The habitat enhancements (over 20,000 plantings of trees and shrubbery) have in fact aided the upland game on his Kansas farmland. It also benefits Steve, because there is more game available for hunting by his family and friends.

He, along with his two Pointers, is able to roam the land and enjoy some very good upland game hunting. In Kansas, he even harvests a limit of birds now and then.

It is his opinion that he can roam Minnesota with his pointers, get a lot of exercise, but not see any game. This may be an exaggeration, but the general trend in Minnesota is downward when it comes to quail, pheasants and waterfowl. In fact, quail are all but extinct in Minnesota.

Steve hunts deer in Minnesota. Even though he hunts, he never has been overly thrilled or excited with deer hunting.

I believe Steve likes the excitement he feels when his dogs go on point, and when a bird flushes. He, using his 20 gauge O/U shot gun, now has a chance to harvest a bird.

Most of us would agree that a flushing bird, when you're hunting upland game, is an exciting moment. When you compare a hunter flushing a pheasant or a covey of quail, to that of his sitting on a deer stand for hours, hoping you might see a deer; one can understand why he prefers bird hunting to deer hunting.

Several years ago, even, Steve had a decent day while deer hunting. He was using a stand his dad had set up several years earlier. The stand is known in our camp as one that each year produces a deer or two.

Chapter 26
A True Bird Hunter
Steve Sjodin

To me deer hunting has always been very boring. I would sit in a stand and wait. Then after a little while I would wait some more. Guess what, after a few more hours, I could wait some more.

I would sit in my stand and think about bird hunting. I love hunting waterfowl and upland game. I have two dogs, both are pointers, they are excellent bird dog's.

As I'm sitting there I keep wondering why I am doing this 'thing' called deer hunting. I could be in Kansas pheasant, turkey or quail hunting and seeing some action.

This did not happen only once, over the years it has happened many times. Once in a while I do harvest a deer. It is exciting for a few hours but then you go back out and sit and you wait, you wait some more and finally it is time to go back to camp. Thank God, I can go back to the cabin and relax and see if anybody else had any luck.

It was opening day in 2007. The day started out just like every other opening morning. Out of bed around 4:40 to 5 am, get dressed and have breakfast. Nothing was new in the procedure.

It was the same old opening morning ritual as all the other opening days. After a breakfast of SOS and some coffee I put on my blaze orange hunting clothes. Soon I am starting up my all-terrain vehicle and motoring out to the stand I would use that morning.

It is a stand that my dad set up seven or eight years earlier. It was going to be available on opening day. I decided to use it. It had a better track record than the stand I had been using.

This stand is located just east of the creek, about a mile from our cabin. There is a large beaver dam with a large pond on the south side of the dam. It is a natural crossing point for deer traveling east or west. The stand is located in a prime area and the deer use the beaver dam when crossing the creek. From the stand I had good visibility. I could see several hundred yards in both, north and south, directions.

As I was starting my propane heater I again was wondering why I'm even out of here. Over a two day weekend last year I shot three deer, a doe and two bucks, a six and 10 pointer. I usually don't shoot many deer at least not that many. I usually just sit and wonder why I'm even here.

The way it usually goes it will be another five years before I even see a deer. At least that's been my history.

I sit in my stand listening to the ducks and geese in the beaver pond. As I do I started wondering why I'm not in a duck blind or out walking some fields back in Kansas.

Oh well at least I'm warm now days when I'm deer hunting. I placed my heater on a shelf under the floor. Earlier I had cut a hole in the floor of the stand so the heat would rise up into the stand. As the heat rises my consolation for me is; there's no more being 'cold' in my stand!

But as I was sitting and dreaming of duck hunting I spotted a deer moving toward me. I will let him cross the creek so I don't have to drag him too far. Okay, he's close enough, I shoot and down he goes.

Oh wait, there is a second deer standing near the spot where the first deer was standing when I shot. I take a shot and down he goes. Boy two deer within minutes of each other on opening day.

So now I wait my 'self-imposed 20 minutes' before I leave my stand and go and field dress the downed deer. I reached the closest one and start the work of field dressing the animal. When I finished the field dressing I started looking for the second deer.

I knew it should be very close to the one I just finished field dressing. I made a big circle through the area and did not find any blood trail. No sign of the second deer could be found.

I went back and took a good look at the first deer. When I rolled him over I found two bullet paths in the deer that I had field dressed. Obviously there was no second deer.

The first deer that I had dropped must have stood up and my second shot was as accurate as the first. There went my thoughts of two deer early on opening day.

After that little disappointment I dragged my deer closer to my stand and propped him up so he could cool down. At least I had a nice looking six pointer.

Several hours go by and it's nearing lunchtime. Before I could break out my lunch I spotted a second deer coming across the same beaver dam that my six pointers used. I again waited for him to cross the creek.

In my mind I'm urging this deer to hurry up and turn broadside. Then I could take a good shot.

Finally he's in position and I take a shot and hit him in the lungs. To my surprise he's still standing there. I took a second shot that I placed in his neck. Down he goes. I can see him lying there; again I waited 20 minutes before I go down to field dress the animal.

During the 20 minutes I take the time to eat my lunch. It was a sandwich Charlie made to my specifications the night before. It was a meat and cheese sandwich along with some cookies. After lunch I was ready to go to work again and field dress my second buck.

Again I'm thinking that's pretty nice, two bucks on opening day. I'm a really happy hunter! After field dressing him and dragging him back to my stand I laid him next to the first one. This one was bigger than the first and he was an eight pointer.

Okay, I am back in my stand and looking forward to a boring afternoon. Soon four more hours have gone by and it has been a real boring afternoon; even the ducks and geese are quiet. A little more time goes by and now it's about time for the sun to set; leaving a half hour before the end of shooting hours.

I started feeling that basically today I've had a pretty good day of deer hunting. I was actually thinking that it's been a very good day. Not very many of us harvest two bucks on opening day.

I checked my watch and I was down to 20 minutes left for today's hunting. Maybe I should leave early. I didn't, the next time I checked I had 10 minutes to go; the next time I checked I only had five more minutes to left.

I was starting to look around to see what I needed to pack up as headed back to camp. As I was looking my first thought was 'Oh my God' it is another deer. He just stepped out of the woods, again on the far side of the beaver dam. Is he going to come across?

Well, I can see he has horns, a lot of them and they are big. I better shoot now; it will soon be too dark and past shooting hours. I don't want to chase him in the dark so I took another neck shot.

I shot and I did not see him run, fall or anything. I knew the tree he was near when I shot. So I waited about 20 minutes before I headed over to start looking and/or whatever I would have to do. That was a long wait especially as it was getting darker in the woods.

When I reached the tree, I had spotted, there was no need for looking; my third buck was dead. Right there where I figured he'd be, one shot in the neck at about 110 yards. A nice shot even if I say so myself.

The grass was very tall across the creek so I never saw him fall. But I knew he did have a nice rack; this deer was a 12 pointer. Boy, now I was happier than I was earlier in the day. This was the biggest buck I had ever shot. Okay, it was now time to get the knife out and collect another heart for camp.

Earlier I had heard everyone else on their four wheelers driving back to camp. I knew I needed help to get the three bucks back to camp. I packed up, jumped on my four wheeler and headed back to camp. When I arrived there I was the last one who returned to camp.

When I got in, they, (my father Jr., Charlie, Chuck and the others) asked if I had shot a deer. I said no; 'I got 26 total points'. It got so quiet you could have heard a pin drop. Everybody's jaw had suddenly dropped.

As I looked around the cabin my Dad was glowing with pride. He had the biggest smile I have ever seen. Now, I realized, that's why I go deer hunting.

Steve Quade, my brother Dan and I drove back with a trailer to get my three deer. First we had to drag the 12 pointer the 30 yards over the beaver dam. We then put all three bucks in the trailer and headed back to camp.

Boy, when we got back to camp everybody was happy for me. Everybody was exclaiming 'wow' 26 points. The 12 pointer really topped it all off.

After harvesting three bucks in one day I was one happy hunter. Never had I had as many deer hunting opportunities in a season as I had the seasons of '06 and 07. Now I had taken three bucks in one day. It was an unbelievable and exciting day of deer hunting for me.

The three deer had 26 total points between them on their antlers. Banner days like the one I had in 2007 are hard to come by.

Maybe I'll get another opportunity on another hunt. Just maybe I should have stayed a few more days than I did. I probably could have harvested another three bucks.

I would love to do that so I could 'over throw' my uncle, "The Buck King." My uncle Punky claims to be the "Buck King" at the Lean-To-Boys hunting camp. I guess he is and he earned it when he harvested five bucks one year. But I really think it would be fun to de-thrown him.

After five decades, it is time for a new "Buck King". That thought will get him thinking. He probably will go out and raise the number to six or so, who knows. In the meantime I'll have to be happy with the three bucks in one day that I harvested in 2007. At least it made me 'The Buck King for the Day'

I want you to know my having one or two good days hunting deer doesn't mean I'll give up bird hunting. No way, my giving up bird hunting will not happen.

I still love the thrill of working with my two pointers. When my pointers are 'on point' and I give them the 'ok' for them to flush the bird and then a nice big rooster pheasant rises out of the grass the thrill is hard to beat.

When the pointers flush a covey I get my chance to warm up my 20 gauge O/U shotgun. The whole experience is still a wonderful thrill, one that I can repeat several times each day. That would be an awful exciting bunch of thrills to give up, so I won't.

More than likely on the opening weekend of every deer season I'll leave my dogs at home. You'll find me in a stand sitting and waiting, sitting and waiting and reliving in my thoughts that opening day in 2007. Just maybe I'll have another banner year, if not; I know I did have one that was special in 2007.

Charlie's Notes: That opening day Steve harvested three bucks with a total of 26 points on their antlers. In my life I have never seen Steve more animated and excited than I did that day. To top it off he won, with one of his bucks, our camps 'kitty' for the biggest buck that opening day. As luck would have it, I was the only other hunter who harvested a buck that day. Mine, at best was only in 2nd or 3rd place.

Good luck Steve on your quest to become "The LTB's Buck King."

Note: Chapter # 26 was used to high light Steve's 26 point day in 2007.

Chapter 27

STANDS

Charlie Turnbull

To us, they are an important part of the deer hunting we do. As you can see, they do not have to be pretty. More and more, however, we are improving their appearance.

In 1952, we did not have or use stands as we know them today. We sat on rocks, stumps, logs, tree limbs or the ground.

That worked for us back then. As we have been improving our hunting skills, we have come to rely heavily on stands,.

Even without stands, as we know them today, we were successful that first year. We filled our four tags and had venison on our plates the next week.

Compared to the early 1950s, our use of stands has come a long way. At this time, we look at "stands" as an important component in our yearly planning and hunting experience.

As we use them today, a stand needs to meet several basic criteria. First, it must be in a productive location. Second, it must be safe. And third, it must be comfortable.

First

The location selected has to be in a productive area. Location, location and location is what determines value in real estate transactions. That same principle holds true in selecting a place for your deer hunting stand.

Selecting a productive location for your stand is crucial. Scouting the area before the season opens is needed. Identifying the deer crossings, bedding areas and where the deer feed are all part of the scouting process.

If these factors are not taken into consideration, your success ratio will be diminished. In fact, you just may not see any deer. If you want a lesson in futility, build a stand in an area that the deer do not use. Without any deer showing up, it is rather difficult to be successful in harvesting one.

When looking for a productive area, watch for natural shooting lanes. In our area, we have used survey lines and logging roads as natural places to establish stands. They offer us wide, natural shooting lanes, often, in the thickest wooded areas.

We have identified three or four survey lines over the years. By walking the survey lines or the logging roads, you can find the natural places where deer cross them on a regular basis. When you have found several likely deer crossings on a logging road or a survey line, you also have built-in shooting lanes.

Second

Safety starts with the hunter and the eventual location of his stand. Above, I suggested using logging roads and/or survey lines as possible places to look for a good location for a stand. They do offer some drawbacks when safety is considered.

When using them for a hunting stand location, you have a greater responsibility to watch for others who may walk them as they are hunting or otherwise enjoying the outdoors. On any stand, "target identification" is important.

I know a person whose 16-year old friend was shot as he sat in a tree stand. The offending hunter did not properly identify his target. After that, my friend gave up deer hunting. It was a sad story and a sad reason for him to give up hunting. Each of us has a responsibility to be more than doubly alert and aware when hunting and handling firearms.

Now that you know where you will build your stand, another safety factor comes into play. How you build or buy the stand is equally important. Build it so it is safe and sturdy. If you buy one, make sure that it is sturdy and that it will accommodate two people.

We know from experience that falling out of a tree is not good. In the late 1950's, Clarence proved that when he went to sleep and fell from a tree. From the fall, he suffered a compression fracture in his back. A tree limb doesn't cut it for safety reasons.

Third

The third is the level of comfort that the hunter wants in his stand. To be a successful deer hunter, we feel that staying on a stand is very important. We know as our kids started hunting with us that the more comfortable they were, the longer they stayed in their stands. Comfort as we see it is having a good seat, a propane heater, a roof on the stand to keep the snow and rain off, a stainless steel thermos bottle for coffee or hot chocolate, some snacks and something to read.

At this time in our deer hunting, we rely about 90% of the time on stands. We rely on them 100% during the first four hours on opening morning.

We have found that, over the years, we have a reasonably good idea how and where the deer move in our hunting area. Our stand locations reflect that knowledge and experience.

Even so, we scout the area around our stands to make sure that the deer are using the trails. Each year, we clear the unwanted grass and brush. If we find problems, we make the needed adjustments. We also relocate our stands when needed.

As we were aging, or have aged, as several of us have done, we have learned that it is easier to let the deer do the walking. So, go scouting and find their trails, build a good stand, and wait for the deer to come to you. It is so much easier that way.

On occasion, new beaver dams change the deer's travel routes in our hunting grounds. The dams force the deer to change their travel routes. In turn, we have to make the needed changes to our stand locations.

In Itasca County, they let out contracts for logging. When they do, the countryside changes and we, again, need to regroup. In 2012, I came to my stand and the nearby timber had recently been harvested. My shooting lanes were lost. After thirty-five years, I had to make some real changes.

One hunting party that hunts the area north of us was using deer stands when we first started hunting the Bigfork area back in 1952. In their area, they had a stand on every corner of their logging roads. Most of their stands had old army blankets for sides. Most were totally enclosed and they had "shooting ports" that they could use when a deer presented itself.

Another one of their hunters back in the 1950's climbed up and into an evergreen tree and had developed a fairly comfortable perch. He had found a grassy area in the woods where the deer bedded down. He would usually be on stand first thing in the morning. He was quite successful in filling two or three licenses for their party.

What he had was a productive area overlooking a natural bedding area and several trails. His shooting lanes were safe, he was in an area with no logging roads or survey lines and he could clearly see anyone walking through his field of view. His level of comfort met his needs; for me sitting on limbs did not look that comfortable. For him, his level of productivity offset any comfort problems.

Another party in our area made a ladder out of an evergreen tree that they had cut down. They cut off the branches in such a way that the heavier ones stuck out from the trunk about 6" to 12." They could use that evergreen tree (ladder) to climb up and into any nearby tree. The problem I saw with that makeshift ladder was the need to be an acrobat. I think it could rotate with me halfway up the tree.

The system evidently worked for them because we found that arrangement in several places throughout the woods. That so-called ladder and a single board nailed up in the tree to sit on was the only evidence of their use of the area.

The biggest problem with most of us is taking the time needed to do a good job of building a deer stand. It takes some preparation to put together a stand. With some preplanning and purchasing of the materials you need, a good stand can be created.

One thing we know is that deer hunters are not afraid to use their imagination when they are creating a stand in the location they want to hunt. If, however, we would take the time, we could have better and more productive stands in our hunting area.

Stands not only offer us comfort; they increase our opportunity to harvest a deer. When we can set out in the woods all day, we have a much better chance of success. We know deer have patterns they tend to follow during the course of the day. However, they do come through at various other times of the day. The trick is to be in the stand when they come into one of your shooting lanes.

Most of the time a deer, will stop when it comes to a shooting lane, and it will look up and down it. This is especially true when you have snow on the ground and the hunter has walked down that lane, or when the grasses (if there is no snow) are clipped. When a deer comes to a cleared lane, they stop to look things over. That curiosity works in our favor.

The use of stands is becoming an issue in hunting. This is particularly true when hunters are using public lands, or the private lands of others. Years ago, too many of us used the available trees when we built our stands. Now, there is a push to leave the trees alone; particularly, not to pound nails into the trees.

More and more we are moving to free standing stands where we hunt. The stand pictured earlier is free-standing.

This is not only an environmental issue; it is also an economic issue. When the lumberjacks and sawmills come across logs with nails in them, they are not happy. The nails and other steel items found in logs break their equipment and force them to spend time repairing it.

As sportsmen and hunters we have to honor their needs, too. If we are better stewards of the land, we will have much better luck keeping our forests open to hunting.

Chapter 28

SHELTERS FOR THE LEAN-TO-BOYS

Charlie Turnbull

The original four-man hunting party created its first camp in 1952. Its shelter was a simple lean-to. In 1955, a lean-to again was used; the party henceforth became known as the Lean-To-Boys. Over those 60 or more years the Lean-To-Boys have used many combinations of shelters.

When you have been hunting as a party for that length of time, you start to know a lot about evolution. Over the past 60 years, our shelters have gone through an evolutionary process. I suspect the process will continue.

When I talk about evolution, I am not talking about how it applies to the development of man. I'm talking about changes in our selection and the development of the various shelters for our camp. Our shelters have gone from very basic, you might say primitive, to a fairly comfortable cabin in the woods.

The way we have used shelters, and progressed and even regressed was a part of our lore. I highlighted five distinct eras in the development of our shelters. The first was the lean-to era. It was an era from 1952-1958. The second was the fish house era, which lasted from 1959-1965. The third, was the era of the first cabin, it lasted from 1965-1991. The fourth was the squad tent era, lasting from 1992-1999. The fifth and current is the second cabin era, started in 1999.

The first cabin era, 1965 to 1991, represented twenty six years of enjoyment. Each of the five eras had some positives. Obviously, some of the eras had more negatives than one would like. When you don't care for something, or like what you have, you look for changes. Looking for something better or something that works is what the creation of our eventual shelter has been all about. Creating something better, based on better and/or more affordable ideas, is a form of evolution. God knows we did that many times.

The Lean-To era 1952-59

Junior and I are the only two who have lived through all of the changes. Leon and Punk are close behind. In 1952, we used a lean-to for our basic shelter.

Another hunting party in 1952, whom we named the Post Office Party, was hunting in the same area we were. They were aware of the type of shelter we used in 1952.

That same party was hunting in the area in 1955 when Junior, Leon and Punky set up their lean-to. At that time, the other party was using a fish house for its shelter. Because of the bitter cold in 1955, they let the three Lean-To-Boys warm up in their heated fish house.

The Post Office hunting party coined the term "Lean-To-Boys" for our hunting party. Since that time, we have become known as the Lean-To-Boys throughout the Bigfork area. We still refer to the other party as the Post Office party.

The lean-to we used in 1952 was probably the most primitive of all. It only had 8 to 10 poles leaning on a cross bar with a canvas draped over them. The sides were wide open. The front too, as you would expect, was open.

The first year, we were fortunate and had fairly mild weather. If it had rained or snowed, we probably would have been very miserable and cold hunters. We were lucky that the weather held for us all weekend.

The lean-to we used in 1955 was a lot better in terms of the canvas for the sides and roof. Junior and his two brothers were fairly well prepared. He had been taught over the years by his father how to survive in some very cold weather.

The knowledge he had gained from his father served them well in 1955. One of their first priorities was to establish a means of heat. Junior always said that having matches (lightly covered with paraffin and kept in a waterproof container) and a good candle means you can always get a fire started. That lesson from his father served them well in ten below zero weather.

The Fish House Era 1959-65

The fish house era basically lasted from 1959-65. We call it the fish house era, although, it would be best if we called it the "Fish House and Tent era." The fish house was used for cooking and eating. The tent, which was pitched directly behind the fish house, was where we slept.

The fish house we used in 1959 was hauled up north on a trailer. There were only four of us hunting. We were able to have four bunks built into it. It was only a 6' x 8' shelter mounted on a trailer, but we made it work very well for our party of four.

1959 was a cold year, with temperatures often reaching 10 to 30 degrees below zero. The fish house not only provided us with bunks, it offered us a confined area that we could heat. Being able to get out of the cold was a real bonus the first week end in 1959.

In 1960, we again used a fish house. We took it to Bigfork in five sections that were piled on a trailer. When we arrived at camp, all we had to do was put the five pieces together. We used a tarp for the floor.

The design was such that the corners had interlocking clips, and all you needed to do was slide the two clips together. The roof rested on top of the four sides, and it was secured with a hook and eye system.

The fish house, which we used from 1960-65 for shelter, was only 8' x 8'. After a year or two, we had to wrap it in tar paper or we would have lost it to rot. After 1965, it was used for storage. For many years the fish house became a valuable part of our shelter system, and we were able to use it for sleeping, staying warm and cooking. It even lasted for several years after the first cabin was built. After the first cabin was built, the fish house was used primarily for storage. Eventually it was moved from our campsite.

The First Cabin Era 1965-91

Punky, who was a carpenter, decided it was time to build a more permanent shelter to replace the fish house and tent. At his job sites, he started scrounging building materials that the other carpenters were discarding. Over a period of time, he had enough building materials, including windows and other supplies to build a 12-by-16 foot cabin. The cabin was built in the fall of 1965. Punky and his friend, Bob, took on the job.

The first cabin era lasted from 1965-91, about 26 years. The cabin was built behind and next to the fish house. In that way, we could go directly back and forth between the cabin and the fish house.

The first cabin was only 12' x 16' and very basic. On the 12-foot east wall six bunks were built-in during construction. The kitchen stove was over on the west wall. There was some storage and counter space on both sides of the stove. The woodstove was near the south wall, properly spaced and placed in the middle.

The table and chairs were between the woodstove and the north wall. People in the real estate business would call it a "great room." We saw it as a "great shelter." The cabin's main door was on the east end of the south wall. Another entrance was on the east end of the north wall. It exited into the fish house.

To build the cabin, Punky and Bob did the layout. They did the hammering and assembly of the materials that Punky had acquired for the cabin. Junior and Doug had the job of bringing the materials from the minimum maintenance road to the camp.

The end result was a very comfortable shelter for the six hunters in our camp in the middle 60s. Many of us have always felt the first cabin era was the best.

As time went on, several other hunters joined our party. Within several years, our party had grown to 10 and then 12 hunters. The cabin and the old fish house at that time were no longer adequate.

Our evolutionary trend continued. The cabin was expanded another 8 x 16 feet on the back side. Additional bunks were built into the addition. As these new needs dictated, we had gone through another evolutionary change.

When we first started using the cabin, our lighting source was one or two Coleman lanterns. We added the use of an overhead propane gas light. At that time, we were able to have a gas cook stove, too.

As time went on, little improvements were made. We started using a generator for our lights. Paul and Leon added the cedar shingles to the exterior and the cabin.

By 1991, things were looking very good. The doors to our cabin were never locked. Over the years, we never had any major incidents involving damage or theft. It was a remarkable period of time for our Bigfork hunting story.

Our cabin was also meaningful to many other people. The local snowmobile maps listed our cabin as a warming shack for snowmobilers. It also had a reputation amongst area teen-agers as a great place for "making out." We never were able to totally substantiate that rumor.

A couple of young people we knew would not, when asked, confirm or deny it.

The cabin was actually positioned in a central location. The cabin's location was back in the woods, and, from it we had easy access to and from our stands.

With our new "off the road" vehicles, we easily moved throughout the area. Any move in the direction of the minimum maintenance road only made access to our stands and hunting areas more time-consuming.

At that time, we had a high level of comfort in our cabin and its location. Several times we asked ourselves, "With this cabin and our good hunting, what more could you ask for?"

The answer came in the fall of 1991. Leon received a letter from the area Forester advising us to remove our cabin. If we did not comply with his ultimatum the cabin would be burned.

We were what one may call "squatters" on government land. There was no way to deny the fact we were squatters. With that letter, we became "very sad squatters."

The question was how we would deal with this major problem. A work party for the middle of January 1992 was organized. We gutted the cabin and removed everything of value. It was a sad day for our Lean-To-Boys that year. The end of the first cabin era was the end of a way of hunting.

Later on, Junior found out that a phone call to a local logger might have saved the cabin. Hindsight is wonderful but not always helpful. So far, the "first cabin era" has been our longest one.

Junior and I spent time discussing the situation. Building another cabin on government land would be taking a major risk. We needed to purchase some land for a cabin.

Buying land was a viable option. Junior and I were stable enough financially to back such a move. The question of financing the purchase of land wasn't the problem. The problem was finding a suitable piece of land to purchase.

One of our hunters had a large acreage adjacent to the area we hunted. Punky and I approached him and asked if he would sell us one acre for a new cabin.

We were prepared to pay a premium price for 1 acre. Punky and I felt that the offer we made to him was more than reasonable. For whatever reason, we were turned down. It didn't make any difference why; we were out of luck. We were still operating from our first premise; we needed to buy some land.

The Squad Tent Era 1992-99

Steve, Jim and Jr., are shown, having coffee in the squad tent.

We had been living very well in our first cabin. Without an available cabin, we turned to a "squad tent." This was the start of the Squad Tent Era. It was in the fall of 1992.

A squad tent was big enough for our party. In some ways, it was even more spacious than the cabin. However, it was very hard to heat and was a problem from a maintenance point of view. Erecting the squad tent, taking it down and resetting the bunks required a lot of extra effort. The bunks that had been taken from the cabin had to be remade and stacked two-high each year. The job of doing the work always fell on those people who came early, and those who were leaving last.

The Second Cabin Era 1999-

One season I hunted Saturday to Monday; on Tuesday morning, I did not go out to a stand. I was in bed when Junior came back to camp and woke me up. Junior had returned rather abruptly and he was excited.

He saw several "for sale" signs on a piece of land as he was driving by. The land was a piece that we had put a priority on if it ever did come on the market. He woke me up and told me about the for sale signs. I assured him it would be purchased that day. I would take care of it on my way home.

The night before was a real "comical" experience for all of us. We were sitting around the dinner table Monday night when we heard a car drive down the minimum-maintenance road. It was shortly after 8 P.M. It started everybody speculating as to why the car was out there. As it turned out, nobody had a clue.

Our main thought was that it was a young couple coming out there to "park and make out" or maybe it was even a "poacher." To our surprise that wasn't the case at all. It was the local Bigfork Realtor out there putting up "for-sale" signs on a brand new property he had just listed.

Junior and I split the basic down payment. Several years later we divided the 80-acre parcel into four 20-acre parcels. Junior and I both took a 20-acre parcel; the other two 20's were sold to other members of our hunting party.

Shortly after that purchase, Vince decided to build a second cabin on our 20 acres. He definitely did not like the squad tent as a headquarters for our hunting party.

The fact that he had recently started working for Home Depot aided his decision. There, he was able to design a cabin and buy materials when they were on sale. Because of Vince's decision, the second cabin era was born.

The timing was right for a new cabin as enough variables had fallen into place to make it feasible. We had the land, Vince wanted something better than a tent, and Junior and I were in a position to help do the work. Others of our hunting party also would pitch in from time to time.

Vince started this project in the summer of 1998. For some time, Vince had been purchasing materials for the project. He had worked out a plan for his cabin. It would be a 1½-story structure with two bedrooms on the main floor.

The cabin would be 24' x 30'. The upper area was an open bunk area for some of the newer hunters. The first floor had the living room, dining room and kitchen all in one big 18' x 24' area. In the back, there were two 10' x 12' bedrooms, and between the two bedrooms was the stairway to the second floor.

Vince had selected a place on the 20 acres that was a couple hundred yards east of the minimum maintenance road. When building the cabin several trees were removed so that it could be placed in a nicely-wooded area. The front door faces north. The cabin is elevated 4', providing us with lots of storage space for wood and other supplies.

At this time, the second cabin is our most advanced stage in the evolution of our shelters. It has been working fairly well. To get to our stands, we have to drive at least a mile further. We use the same logging roads today that we used in 1952.

Over the next few years, we will see what time and experience dictate and require us to adjust. For now, we will continue to enjoy a cabin that has an excellent wood heater, comfortable bunks and almost all the comforts of home.

Maybe we do not have all the comforts of home, but, most of them. We still use a nice outhouse. But even the outhouse is better than what we used in the past. Maybe Junior is correct when he says that we've come a long way and we are now "gentlemen hunters."

Chapter 29

EVERY CAMP NEEDS AN OUTHOUSE

Charlie Turnbull

Everywhere that man has lived here on the planet earth, he has had to deal with his excretions. Men can live with their excretions. Not a pleasant thought. A man can hide his waste by covering it up with any object that will cover it. Another alternative is to bury it. You could burn it or even drop it in a body of water.

When there were few men occupying the earth, it did not make much difference which system was used. If it smelled, they could move away from it. Because we have over-populated the planet, people have had fewer options in how they are going to handle human and animal excretions.

At our camp, we have tried several methods over the past 60 or more years. I think it is fair to say that the "Lean-To-Boys" have gone through an "evolutionary" process in this aspect of our hunting and camping experience. It is a process that will probably continue into the future. The following is the basic evolutionary process we used over the last 60 or more years.

In the early years, 1952 to 1959, we usually didn't have a real outhouse. We usually would go away from camp to do our job. Many times, we used the cover-up method. If we had an entrenching tool or another shovel, we would bury our fecal droppings. This worked when our parties were smaller and we were hunting for shorter periods of time.

In 1960, we started having a permanent camp site and we needed a more permanent outhouse arrangement. At first, the arrangement was not elaborate; it did give us a place to sit or do a balancing act while passing our stool.

It was usually a 2" to a 3" limb nailed or tied to two trees that were probably 24 to 30 inches apart. On the other side of the 3" limb, we dug a small hole, one we would fill with dirt before we broke camp. Even if it did work, this was not the most comfortable form of a so-called "outhouse."

It was also the catalyst that pushed us to build a little better outhouse. By this process we were evolving further into our outhouse designs.

The next one involved building a platform out of small limbs so that you could actually sit on it. If you're going to be occupied for a while, we realized it was important to make a cover over your head to keep the rain or snow off when sitting. Of course as soon as we developed the platform that we could sit on and do our job, it became evident that it would be more comfortable if we just added a toilet seat on the platform. That was simple. Just buy one and install it.

One of our hunters, Steve, is shown using the camp's outhouse. It did have a store-bought seat. The rest of the structure is logs with a sheet of plywood on top to keep the rain or snow off while sitting and meditating.

In 1992, we were told to move our cabin from the campsite. We had been squatting on Itasca County land. We had been advised to move our cabin or they would burn the cabin down. This was a real letdown to us and various snowmobilers, people who used it as a warming place in the winter.

The outhouse wasn't a problem anymore. The problem was the shelter we were using. It was a military squad tent. It kept the rain and snow off you and your equipment. The biggest problem with the squad tent was that it was nearly impossible to heat.

Because the squad tent had its problems and life was colder than it needed to be, Vince decided to build a cabin. We had purchased 80 acres in the area. It was a purchase that Junior and I took care of when the land became available. Once we purchased the land, we subdivided the land into four 20-acre parcels.

The 80 acres is on the east side of the northbound section of the "minimum-maintenance road." When we subdivided the land, a ten-foot easement was established. It is along the east edge of the property. In this way, the owners of all four parcels have a travel lane for the half-mile length of the 80 acres.

The two Steves in our party paid for the South 20, Punk took the next 20, Junior took the next one and I took the North 20. Vince opted to put the cabin on our 20 acres.

Building the cabin took a couple of years. During that time, Junior built a very nice outhouse. It had three sides, a roof, a built-in seat and a solid floor. It was built with dimension lumber and several wood doors with windows for the sides. If it had a flaw, it might've been that the entrance was open and facing north.

Shortly after we started using the new cabin, a new hunter, Chuck's son, Frank, joined our party. He had a habit or a need to sit in the outhouse for 30 to 40 minutes every morning. It was not a good situation for us "old salts" during the morning rush hour.

With 12 to 15 hunters in camp, it became evident that we needed a different arrangement. A second outhouse was rapidly built to accommodate Frank. He is the only one with his own private outhouse.

To build it, an A-frame style of construction was used. The A-frame consisted of five boards; plywood for the deck, two plywood pieces for the sides, another sheet of plywood for the back and a board for the seat. It was assembled and built in an unorthodox style, at least unorthodox for an outhouse.

This became Frank's personal biffy. It worked, relieving the pressure for all of us, especially for us "old salts." You know, who they are, the hunters who need a clear path to the outhouse first thing every morning.

Finally, in 2000, Vince built a very good outhouse with "one-hole." It is a 4' x 8' structure. It has four insulated walls, a nice roof, a window that can be opened and a door with a window. The outhouse's deck is plywood. When we are using it, we leave a Coleman lantern burning. It furnishes the light we need and it keeps the outhouse warm and comfortable. To date, it is our "Cadillac" outhouse. The other two are still there in case there's an emergency.

Do I think we have stopped evolving? No way. We do not have indoor plumbing. I assume that at some point there will be indoor plumbing. I suppose at that point the terminology "outhouse" will not be proper terminology for an indoor toilet system. Until then "outhouse" it is.

Note: Reference books you might like to read that are all about outhouses and outdoors elimination.

> The All American Outhouse, Stories, Design & Construction by Bob Cary, A.S. O.A.
> Publisher: Adventure Publications, Inc.
> Cambridge, Minnesota.
> How to Shit in the Woods by Kathleen Meyer
> Publisher; Ten Speed Press
> POB 7123
> Berkley, California, 94707

Chapter 30

THE EVOLUTION OF OUR MEANS OF TRAVEL

Charlie Turnbull

The Lean-To-Boys have had an evolutionary process going on in three major areas. The first was in our use of, and the development of, various shelters. The second form of evolution has been in our outhouses. This chapter is about how we have travel, or how we currently travel to and from our camp and stands.

Over the years, we have used a wide variety of vehicles for transportation. In 1952 we were able to drive our cars all the way to our camp site. There have only been several other years when a car *or truck was able to drive to the camp site.*

Hiking in to our camp has always been an option. It is the most reliable, but the hardest. That, of course, was before some of us became senior citizens. Hiking in is not a good choice for us seniors. In 1955, Junior, Punky and Leon had to walk in to hunt. Their dad, Clarence had made a beautiful sled for them to push and pull. It, too, did not survive the test. It broke down the first time they used the sled.

Over time, the old logging roads have continued to deteriorate. Several massive mud holes have only grown larger. They started out small, but they are deeper and wider now. The mud holes in the wet years impeded access to our camp and deer stands. Another party in the 1950s used an Army surplus Dodge weapons carrier with four-wheel drive to get back to our area. The ruts and damage they did to the logging road were the start of several deep mud holes. The ruts and scars are still there.

Later, we had our own four-wheel drive vehicles, and we added to the depth and length of the mud holes. One problem has been the lack of any major effort on our part to maintain the logging roads. Instead of a maintenance program we opted for different and better vehicles.

For the reasons cited above, we have developed or used all kinds of vehicles to travel to our hunting area. Some did not live up to our expectations. Others were very successful, but for one reason or another faded into the sunset. We have found the evolutionary path takes many turns when we discuss our means of travel.

In several of the earlier hunting trips, we had to walk into the camp. This meant that we used packs and/or we towed a toboggan the 1½ miles to camp. Our need for something better was always highlighted after one of those hikes.

Now almost every one of the Lean-To Boys has their own "off-road vehicle." Some of the vehicles, trailers and other means of transportation are discussed below. Some of our means of transportation were unique answers to meet the problems we encountered. In other cases, vehicles have been purchased right out of a dealer's show room.

The area we hunt always responds to excessive rainfall. In wet years, we have to live with the mud holes in the logging roads.

The first vehicle I want to discuss is one of the first ones we used, and it is pictured in Chapter 10. It was a homemade track style vehicle. It never had a name other than being called "The Swamp Buggy."

It is one Junior designed and built. His neighbor Doug helped him build it. This machine had homemade tracks, and it was made up of many used automobile parts. The power for the Swamp Buggy was from a 1936, 60-hp Ford V-8 Engine. This vehicle had the ability to cross over the creek without a bridge and to go through any mud hole or water it encountered. It had a box that supplies could be carried in; it also could pull the heaviest of our trailers.

Junior and Doug built the machine in 1960, and it was used throughout the 1960s. If I told you the Swamp Buggy was the best vehicle of any we used in the Bigfork area, I don't think anybody in our camp would disagree. The Swamp Buggy's downfall was its engine. When the 1936 Ford V-8 engine gave way a second time, Junior parked the Swamp Buggy.

It was a "ten-year creation," but for our area it was a very good one. It was a sad ending for a very good machine when it was put in storage. After a successful hunt in 1961, we were shown with a loaded "Swamp Buggy" in the <u>Western Itasca Review News Paper.</u>

Snowmobiles were used several times in our travels to and from the cabin. They would have been very good if we had 10 to 12 inches of snow every hunting season. For the most part, they never were a hit for our hunting purposes. Later in the winter season, Junior and other members of our group did a lot of snowmobiling at Bigfork. They also used the cabin on many of their outings. Once the cabin was warmed up, it was the ideal place for a weekend hideaway.

A vehicle Vince and I have used is called a Jim Dandy." Yes, we really do own a "Jim Dandy." It is a commercially-made lawn tractor. It is a beautiful machine, and it is built using a chain drive, very similar in design to an Alice Chalmers W D tractor.

One time, three of us were using the Jim Dandy to pull a loaded trailer to camp. As long as we were on dry ground, everything was fine. As soon as we came to a mud hole, we were in trouble. It required us to unload the trailer and carry the supplies to the other side and then reload it.

Punky is shown on Big Red, one of his favorite machines.

Carrying our gear around mud holes was another motivator for a better means of transportation. Pain and discomfort have always pushed us to look for better ways of traveling to, from and around our camp.

Gradually, we moved to individual machines for each hunter. One of the first was the three-wheel tricycle style of an all-terrain vehicle. These were great little machines, but they also had their drawbacks. In snow, they were less dependable and usually they were useless. Shortly after the initial surge in their sales, they lost favor and were actually taken off the market. On occasion, you might see an "old one" but not very often. Basically they are a dangerous machine to operate.

In some ways, it worked fairly well. It worked fairly well if it was dry and we did not have to contend with waterholes.

Personally, I used one. As I was entering a mud hole one day, I had to give it some gas to move it up and out of the mud. When I gave it the gas, the immediate power surge it created forced it to veer right, and the front tire ran up a tree three feet. I ended up in the mud with my rifle underneath me. I knew it hurt. I found out exactly why several months later. A doctor who was examining an x-ray of my back asked me when I broke my ribs. I immediately knew when I broke my ribs. I now know why my back was so painful for several weeks back then. It was when I was thrown into the mud puddle and ended up on my back under a three-wheeler. My rifle was under me and the bolt on my rifle gave me a hard jolt in the ribs.

Another time, I was using Junior's "Big Red," and I tipped over into a small creek that was coming from a beaver dam and its pond. I was on my way to my deer stand and it was a bitterly cold morning. It was much too cold to have my head under water with the three wheeled all-terrain vehicle resting on top of me. I was happy to push it off me and get my head out of the water. I decided to go to my stand and use the heater I had to dry myself and my clothes.

Incidents like that are all part of our camp's traveling experiences. They are also part of what we call deer hunting.

During that same period of time, the four-wheeled all-terrain vehicle became very popular. You could purchase one in a 2x4 or a 4x4 configuration. The advantage of a 4x4 all-terrain vehicle was the four-wheel-drive feature they offered. They come in a wide variety of machines. The Lean-To-Boys have tried almost all of the various models.

There are usually two factors that dictate the machine a person will buy. The first, of course, are the funds you're willing to invest in a machine. The second is what you really need it for, or why you think you need it.

Many owners use the machines for hunting, fishing, joyriding and for work projects around their home. Some people have equipped them with every accessory available. The owner's goal is to make them more comfortable and/or utilitarian. The buyer's planned use becomes a factor in accessories, too.

In addition, several manufacturers also offer 4x4, 4x6 and 6x6 machines with side by side seating. Some of the six-wheeled machines can be equipped with tracks. One of the advantages of these machines is the box built into the back of the vehicle. I own two of these; a Polaris, Ranger 4x4 and a John Deere 4x6. I use them both for hunting and for hauling equipment, supplies and the gear I need and/or want moved from place to place at camp or on my farm land.

One year, our friendly beavers built several dams downstream, and the water was backed up in both directions. The usual place we crossed the creek was flooded. That year, we used a canoe and a six-wheel floating vehicle to cross the creek. We, also, have used a beaver dam for crossing the creek to or from our camp. It usually takes some work in order to drive over them.

The crown, of a beaver dam, is usually too narrow, and requires some work to safely cross it. We know that for a fact. Vince and I went over the side of the dam once with our "Jim Dandy" and trailer. It turned out to be a very cold baptism for Vince.

The six-wheeled floating vehicle and the canoe we used one year, to cross the overflowing creek, are shown in the photo. We soon found out that the six-wheeled vehicle was not the vehicle for our use at Bigfork.

One thing we all know is that our means of transportation is better today than it was years ago. Years ago, we might walk a mile or two to get to our stand. By the time we reached our stand, we had worked up a first-class sweat.

Now we have very little of that early morning sweating. For this, we have to thank our upgraded means of transportation. When walking, the time it took to reach my stand was approximately 45 minutes. Today, without driving fast, it takes me 15 minutes. When I get to my stand I am dry and ready to hunt.

When you couple our means of transportation with our improved stands and the individual propane heaters we use in our stands, you have a formula for good hunting. Our evolution in this area, over 60 or more years, brought us to a point where our means of travel are comfortable, safe and affordable.

I know people who always want the "good old days." The good old days offer us great topics of conversation; as we get older, it's better to talk about them, than to relive them.

This photo is of Chuck crossing the same beaver dam that Vince went over the side of with the Jim Dandy.

Once in a while, it's fun to wish for the "good old days." That was when you could walk for 45 minutes, arrive at your stand, be wet from a good sweat and be cold and freezing for the next hour or two as you slowly dried out. With that said, I think I'll take a "pass" on "the good old days."

Chapter 31

SIXTY YEARS OF RECOLLECTIONS

In 1952, Clarence, Junior, Bob and I were the first ones who had the privilege of starting our Bigfork hunting party. Our name, "The Lean-To-Boys," became our hunting party's name in the early years. The name started after hunters from the Post Office Hunting Party called us by that name back in 1955. The name stuck, and our party and camp has enjoyed the name ever since.

Of all the hunters who have hunted with us, Junior and I are the only two who have continuously, except for our military service years, been involved from the start. At that time, we were 18 and 19 years old, respectively. We definitely were expecting to be in the military for two to three years. In 1953 and 1954 Junior's dad, Clarence, and several others kept our deer hunting campfires burning.

Because of Junior's longtime commitment to the Lean-To-Boys, he has many stories and highlights to reflect upon. In this chapter Junior, shares several of his memories with you and me.

Chapter 31
60 Years of Recollections
Junior Sjodin

As I look back on the last 60 years of hunting, camping, snowmobiling, four wheeling and hiking the woods east of Bigfork, I am reminded of the people and incidents that have made it a great journey. As one of the founders of our camp it is my pleasure to share them with you.

Our First Cabin

I'll start out with the weekend four of us built our first deer hunting shack. Sometimes we even refer to it as our first cabin.

Over the years we went from lean-tos, to plastic tarps over poles, followed by a variety of shelter creations. When we first started our hunting all of us, more or less, lived from hand to mouth. We did the things needed 'to get by,' things we could afford. We have used basic lean-tos, tents and two or three different fish houses. We used hay, plastic tarps, boughs and anything we thought would insulate us from the cold ground.

In the 1960s a friend of mine developed a system for tying together the walls and roof components for an easy to assemble fish house. The system used a product he named the "Duo Tri Way." With this product I was able to put together an 8'x 8' fish house. This fish house design we modified and it became our cook shed. Behind the newly created cook shed we pitched a tent for our sleeping arrangements.

The cook shed and the tent arrangement was okay. Over time however, the material in the cook shed started to deteriorate. My brother Punky, who was a carpenter, started bringing home scrap lumber from his job sites. Over a period of two years he assembled enough material for a small 12 x 16 cabin. If you ever visit or have visited a construction site you will see a lot of what appears to be wasted material.

In reality it's cheaper, on a big job, for a company to discard damaged or miss cut material. To pay a carpenter to use it would be more expensive. Punky knew we didn't need any fancy wood for our first cabin. He would take the time to salvage it. By doing the salvage work, the materials he needed for the deer shack were virtually free. In effect he paid for the materials with his time and efforts.

The year the cabin was built Punky and his buddy Bob did the construction work. That first cabin we owe to the two of them. Those two boys were working faster than Doug and I could bring the material from the minimum maintenance road to the cabin site.

Doug and I hauled the lumber for the shack with the Swamp Buggy and a trailer. We unloaded and immediately headed back for another load of Punky's material. By the time we returned with the next load the previous load was all in place and nailed together.

The two of them, when we finally returned, would be sitting on a stump having a beer. At that point they'd ask Doug and me, "Where have you guys been?" Or they might ask "What took you so long?" All in all it was a fun day and a great use of my Swamp Buggy.

I do not remember how many loads we made that day. I do know the two boys were faster at assembling the cabin than Doug and I could have done it.

Pictured in front of the fish house in the 1st row are: Junior, Don, and Doug; second row Bob, Charlie and Punky.

The fish house as it was the year prior to building the first cabin.

The original cabin that we built that Saturday in September was 12' x 16'. It had six bunks built into the east wall. Our propane cook stove and cooking utensils ended up on the west wall. Our table was in the north central part of the cabin. We had a small wood stove in the south central part. That first hunting shack was the most comfortable and memorable accommodation we ever have had in over 60 years of hunting the area.

The original cabin was built for a party of six. We had six hunters in camp that 1st year. They were Charlie, Punky, Doug, Don, Bob and I. Each of us had a built-in bunk, a foam mat to sleep on and a warm place where we could sit around the table and enjoy a meal and share some great hunting stories.

A Sauna in the Woods

Coming from Minnesota I knew about saunas. In fact we had one at our cabin on Mabel Lake, west of Remer, Minnesota. There we could take a sauna and merely jump in the lake to cool off. At our deer camp we talked about having a sauna, why not? I asked.

To build it we dug a hole approximately 2' x 2' and 1 foot deep. On top of the hole we build a small 4' x 6' enclosure. The enclosure we built could be closed up to trap the steam that the hot rocks and water would create. To get the steam we just poured water over the extremely hot rocks.

We had two steel cartons, each one held four cartons of milk. Using the steel milk cartons to hold and carry the rocks we heated them over an open fire. We had to rig a carrier with a pole so we could transport the hot rocks back and forth between the sauna and open fire.

It was a simple operation. To those of us who would spend up to two weeks at a time in our hunting camp it gave us a way to take a steam bath. We never had a lake to jump into.

A lake was not available; we just stepped out of the sauna into the cold air. The air was cold enough to cool you off in a big hurry. It was one of those crazy things we did at our camp. It may have been a crazy idea, but what a treat it was for me and the others who were in camp.

A Pit Full of Garbage or 'How to Build a Ground Cannon'

It was mid-September and my boys and I were grouse hunting and using our deer hunting shack. The second day I took the time to look around our campground. To me it looked like we were not taking good care of our area. At least not as good as we should have been taking care of a camping area.

I decided right then and there we needed to dig a garbage pit. That would give us a place to put our garbage and eventually bury it. This would be better than just throwing it here and there.

I told my boys to dig a pit 4'x4'. I didn't tell them how deep to make it. An hour later I checked on their progress. Wow, they had a pit 6' deep. By that time they were filling pails with dirt and hauling the dirt up with a rope. I instructed them to quit digging. The hole which was 6 foot deep was more than deep enough.

By the end of the next year it was almost full of our camps debris. Boxes, paper towels, beer and pop cans and whatever other debris we needed to get rid of filled the hole. On the last day of the deer season I decided it was time to burn the rubbish in the garbage pit.

I found several partially filled cans of oil, stove gas and snowmobile gas to use for starting the fire in the garbage pit. I mixed them together and poured some of the mixture over the garbage and into the pit.

When I threw my lit match into the pit all I heard was a big whoosh. The 6 foot hole had turned into a 'ground cannon.' It was fueled by my exotic mixture of gas and oil that had trickled all the way to the bottom of the pit. It was just waiting for my lit match.

The 'ground cannon's' flaming explosion was Immediate. It literally emptied the pits debris and shot the flaming pieces of paper and cardboard over 20 feet into the cold northern air. The hailstorm of burning papers soon settled all around me. Trees in the immediate vicinity all had burning pieces of paper hanging on them. I had literally decorated them with flaming pieces of paper.

Bob was setting on a stump 100 yards west of the hunting shack. He came running up to see what had happened. His first thought was that it was a 'sonic boom'.

Bob was at one time an airplane mechanic while serving in the United States Navy. During that time he had heard many sonic booms and he knew what caused them. He looked around and soon realized there were no jet airplanes to create a sonic boom.

His second thought was that the propane gas tank for the shack had blown up. To Bob's surprise the shack was still standing. I however was standing in a manmade hailstorm of burning papers.

It was a good thing it was late in the year and we had enough snow. I really did not want to start a forest fire.

When the garbage pit exploded and emptied itself all I heard or felt was a big whoosh. Bob however heard it as a sonic boom. The only thing I could figure out was that I was too close to hear it for what it was.

The one thing we know, it was as loud as a cannon and it made a mess. Obviously there must be a better way to burn a garbage pit.

Wilderness style "Outhouses"

To meet our needs, over the years, we tried several different styles of outhouses. One of the first ones was taking a 3" branch, approximately 4' long and tying it 20" off the ground to two trees. All you had to do was balance yourself when sitting on it.

Obviously comfort was not the object. It soon gave way to an outhouse that was more to our liking.

It was a three sided outhouse with a seat and an open front. If we were expecting inclement weather we only had to throw a tarp over the front to divert the rain or snow. Having a better seat also made it more comfortable.

Our three sided outhouse was a better outhouse at the time it was constructed. Eventually it gave way to what we call our 'Cadillac outhouse.' However, when needed it is still available for our use.

Later on, in a different setting, we developed a fancier outhouse. For us it's the Cadillac of outhouses. Our Cadillac style outhouse has a floor, four walls, a combination storm door, a roof, a nice seat to sit on and a method for heating it.

We have evolved and we have traveled a long way in our efforts to improve and enjoy our hunting and recreation in our camp. A comfortable outhouse is one place where we, too, have come a long way.

The Tinkling Deer Stand

Every once in a while when we're deer hunting something out of the ordinary happens. One day around mid-afternoon I got tired of sitting so I took a walk. I knew one of the guys was sitting on the survey line.

Actually he was close, just a few yards east of it. As I was walking in his direction I kept hearing a metallic tinkling sound. It wasn't what I expected to be hearing. As I got closer the tinkling became louder. I started looking around to find the source of the tangling.

Soon I started seeing beer cans stuck on the ends of many cut off limbs. In total there must've been a couple dozen cans throughout the area. Every time there was a little breeze the cans started their tinkling.

I'm not sure if Bob thought the cans would attract a deer or not. I think his empty beer cans were the only 'trophies' he was able to hang up that year. It was one of those little idiosyncrasies that hunters do to amuse themselves while sitting and waiting for something to happen. Maybe reading a book would have been more productive.

Till the next deer season I'll live with over 60 years of hunting memories. I hope you too have many similar memories. In closing, I want to wish each of you good hunting.

Chapter 32

2012 MINNESOTA DEER HARVEST REPORT

Charlie Turnbull

Table #1 is of the total deer harvest from 1994-2012.

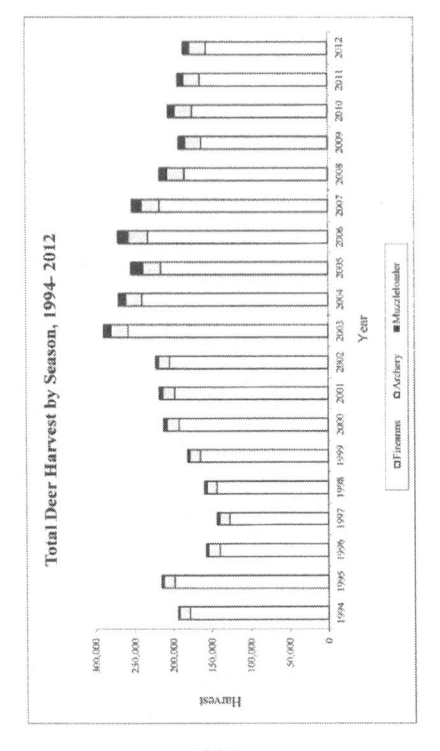

From a low of 150,000 in '97 to a high of 300,000 in '03 the fluctuation in the number of deer harvested is very noticeable. There are 23 tables in the official report.

For more information on the deer herd, success ratios and other hunting information contact the Minn. DNR., 500 Lafayette Road, St. Paul, Minn., 55155-4007

Note: The above information gives you a snap-shot view of how the deer herd changes from year to year. Two, or more, mild winters in a row does more for the herd than anything else. It only takes one severe winter to put a damper on the herd. All I all the DNR has done a good job of keeping the herd in a reasonable balance.